SUN TZU'S

THE ART
OF WAR

OTHER TITLES IN
MEDIA EIGHT BUSINESS CLASSICS

Adam Smith's The Wealth of Nations

Benjamin Franklin's The Way to Wealth

Karl Marx's Das Kapital

George S. Clason's The Richest Man in Babylon

Napoleon Hill's Think and Grow Rich

Miyamoto Musashi's The Book of Five Rings

Frank Bettger's How I Raised Myself from Failure to Success in Selling

MEDIA EIGHT **BUSINESS CLASSICS**

SUN TZU'S

THE ART
OF WAR

TIMELESS Concepts for TODAY

CALUM ROBERTS

This edition published in 2012 by

Media Eight International Publishing Limited

3 Linkside, New Malden,
Surrey KT3 4LA, United Kingdom

Tel: +44 (0)20 8605 1097

ISBN: 978-81-7314-280-2

Printed in India by Gopsons Papers Ltd.

CONTENTS

INTRODUCTION

Yeah, yeah, I know you've heard all about *The Art of War* – what self-respecting business person hasn't, right? Chances are you are among millions around the world who already own a copy, probably strategically positioned at eye level on your bookshelf alongside *On Becoming a Leader* by Warren G. Bennis, *7 Habits of Highly Effective People* by Stephen Covey and *Think and Grow Rich* by Napoleon Hill. And chances are, that like so many of those millions, you sat down one day, excited and enthusiastic to read the wisdom recorded in its ancient pages, only to find that after a few short chapters you'd lost the will to live. Don't worry, your secret's safe with me.

Make no mistake, *The Art of War* is a classic and warrants our deepest respect but it's no easy read – and certainly not for busy professionals who simply don't have the time to pore over the pages and attempt to interpret the meaning and adapt it to their own circumstances. It doesn't help that there are over thirty annotated versions of the book in print today, not to mention countless interpretations regarding particular areas of life, including business strategy, leadership, sporting excellence and – disturbingly – relationships!

The Art of War was of course also originally written in Chinese. As any translator will tell you, the mere act of translation always loses some of the nuances of the original text simply because there is often no exact word or phrase that fully captures the meaning from the original language. Add to that the fact that it was written in the sixth century BC by a Chinese military genius – Sun Tzu or Master Sun, as he was also known – and it's no wonder it's a bit tricky at times.

Yet, despite all that, *The Art of War* is still regarded as essential reading for global entrepreneurs seeking to master strategy and has had a huge influence on military planning both in the East and West.

A bamboo scroll version of *The Art of War* discovered by archaeologists in 1972 confirmed that the treatise consists of only thirteen chapters, each one devoted to one element of successful warfare.

Assuming you don't necessarily have any countries to invade or plan to lay siege to any kingdoms in the foreseeable future, I'll be interpreting the strategy for the debatably less dangerous pursuit of business.

During the course of this book, direct quotations from *The Art of War* will appear in *italics*. The translation I will be using was made by Lionel Giles in 1910. There are many such translations but this one has stood the test of time and while the phrasing may vary from version to version, the essence of what is being expressed is the same.

I would not flatter myself by implying this book is a substitute for the original. Its purpose is simply to illustrate the timeless nature of Master Sun's extraordinary insights by bringing them to life through business case studies.

I hope this format helps to transform the undeniable wisdom contained in the original work into an entertaining accompaniment to one of the greatest books ever written. After all, two and a half thousand years from now, it's unlikely that people will still be poring over *The Da Vinci Code* convinced that a sacred secret lies buried within its pages, or avidly reading any of today's business books in the hope of fast-tracking their career, or seeking advice from a ghost-written book by a daytime TV-guru. But they *will* probably still be reading *The Art of War*.

YOUR PHILOSOPHY MATTERS

Be the change you wish to see in the world.
- GANDHI

Master Sun expounds the Moral Law that requires the people to place unflinching faith in their leader, thereby infusing their lives with the vision of the leader. In business, it refers to company philosophy or corporate values. When this law is strong, it is a living expression of the corporate mission and demonstrated by the corporate culture. A man that has masterfully transferred his own creed and life philosophy into his business and built a formidable empire as a result is Richard Branson. Virgin is the personification of Branson himself – a mischievous, never-say-die, challenger to the status quo. His focus on having fun, a concept not traditionally associated with business, is inherent in everything he gets involved in.

Because of his philosophy, Branson has attracted similar high-energy people whose vision becomes his vision, which they pursue with as much passion, excitement and enthusiasm as he would himself. While many of the Virgin companies are no longer owned or controlled by Branson, the Virgin brand is so valuable and strong that the culture endures even when merged with a larger entity. Often, it is this intangible vibe that attracts interested parties seeking access to markets they can't reach.

FOOD FOR THOUGHT

Thinking about your business or workgroup, take a piece of blank paper and create two columns. In the first column, write five words or phrases that describe the philosophy or *Moral Law* of your business as it is right now. In the second column, write five words or phrases that describe how you would like your business to be. Consider the decisions and actions you have taken recently and see which list you are most demonstrating in your daily business activity.

Traditionally, when you think of business, you think of pinstripe suits and stiff upper lips but neither are found in a Virgin company. Take Virgin Mobile in Australia, for example. They don't have boring old quarterly reviews and there are no dull presentations, PowerPoint or otherwise. Instead, to commemorate a quarter dedicated to taking measured risks and being inspired by new opportunities, selected directors and managers were invited to demonstrate their commitment by taking a few risks of their own. The group had to work together to allocate dares, including learning how to trapeze, holding a tarantula in a spider cage, swimming with sharks, abseiling and aerobatics. Each dare was recorded and shared with the team. Of course, the business side of things was also covered but it was done with flair, passion and fun.

Richard Branson has an incredible ability to attract and keep very entrepreneurial and creative individuals who will willingly sacrifice a higher salary to be involved with the Virgin brand and all that it stands for.

According to the corporate website, *'The Virgin brand is built on Richard Branson's core philosophy – if you keep your staff happy then your customers will be happy, and if you keep your customers happy then your shareholders will be happy.'*

Branson demonstrates perfectly a leader who has harnessed *Moral Law* and infused his people with his own goals.

YOUR THOUGHTS

KNOW YOUR ENVIRONMENT

What a man believes may be ascertained,
not from his creed, but from the assumptions
on which he habitually acts.
- GEORGE BERNARD SHAW

In a business context, this refers to the importance of knowing the market you operate in and understanding the cultural and environmental nuances that apply. Getting it wrong can be costly both to reputation and bottom-line results.

Open any kitchen cabinet in millions of Western homes and you're likely to find a Kellogg's product. After a boom run in the 1980s, growth slowed. In an effort to combat this, Kellogg's looked outside their traditional markets. They plumped for India – excited by a population approaching a billion, a quarter of whom were considered potential customers. It was a brave new world for Kellogg's – except for one tiny detail: people in India generally started their day with a bowl of hot vegetables. Not only would Kellogg's need to educate people about their products but they also needed to change cultural habits so that their products were relevant. Kellogg's didn't understand the terrain. They were blinded by the population figures and the potential upside. In their enthusiasm to get Cornflakes into the Asian market, they conveniently ignored the fact that the target customers didn't eat breakfast cereal and even if they did, only 10% would be able to afford it.

FOOD FOR THOUGHT

Choose an area in your business that is undergoing change – perhaps there is a restructure or you're developing a new product or service. Challenge all the assumptions you've made about your decision. If there is no solid evidence for why you should be pursuing this course of action then someone's made an assumption about its relevance. Instead, go to the environment that will be affected by your actions and ask questions.

WORDS OF WISDOM

The second and third constant factors that govern victory are Heaven and Earth. Heaven and earth are what Sun Tzu refers to as the environmental conditions and the physical terrain of battle, and one must be aware ahead of time of the threats and opportunities that they present.

Similarly, when Gerber took their baby food to Africa, they didn't do some basic research. No doubt to save money, they used the same packaging as for Western markets, which showed a happy smiling baby. But Gerber didn't understand the terrain … In Africa, due to the illiteracy problem, it was common practice for manufacturers to illustrate the contents by printing a picture on the label rather than just relying on the words alone. No wonder sales were low!

In 1988, General Electric Company (GEC) and Plessey joined forces to create a new telecommunication giant. A brand was sought that evoked technology and innovation. Ironically, the chosen name demonstrated neither. The new company was called GEC-Plessey Telecommunications or GPT for short. This seemingly innocuous name was, however, greeted with great hilarity in France; said quickly, the acronym sounded like 'J'ai pété' – or, for those non-French readers, 'I've farted'!

Along the same lines, a Scandinavian vacuum cleaner manufacturer made a marketing faux pas when they launched their product in the United States with the strapline 'Nothing sucks like an Electrolux'. Ouch!

It's important to understand your market and take a walk in your customers' shoes. If you don't, the results can be costly and embarrassing.

YOUR THOUGHTS

FOSTER LEADERSHIP VIRTUES

Leadership is a combination of strategy and character.
If you must be without one, be without the strategy.
- GENERAL NORMAN SCHWARZKOPF

Master Sun makes many references to the importance of the leader and states the virtues of wisdom, sincerity, benevolence, courage and strictness as hallmarks of leadership excellence. Ricardo Semler stands out as displaying all of these characteristics, although not in the stereotypical way. Semler is the head of Semco, a Brazilian business currently involved in manufacturing, professional services and high-tech software. What the business does, however, is secondary to how it does it. There is none of the usual structure of conventional business, no organisation chart or mission statement, no policies and procedures, no planning, no managers, no HR department, no head office, no secretaries and if you want a coffee, you get it yourself. The company doesn't even have a fixed CEO. People decide how much they should be paid and who they want to work with and they don't plan ahead by any more than six months.

When Ricardo joined the family business, he and his father clashed. In an amazing display of courage, his father transferred his shares to his twenty-one-year-old son and went on holiday. By 6 p.m. the same day, Ricardo had fired 60% of Semco's senior management. Since then, Semco has

---

FOOD FOR THOUGHT

Choose a project that is not progressing and apply Semler's 'three whys'. First, approach the person responsible and seek clarification on the delay. That person will probably give a standard response without much thought. Instead of accepting it, question the response for a more considered answer. Repeat again until you get to the source of the hold-up. Take action to either correct the problems or shelve the project.

turned the traditional business model on its head and become not only a remarkable social experiment but an extraordinary success.

The company has gone from a few hundred employees to over 3,000. Despite a fluctuating Brazilian economy, annual revenue grew from $35 million to $160 million between 1994 and 2001. So why does it work?

Firstly, Semler has an 'added 30% faith in human nature'. He believes that if you treat people like adults and give them an opportunity to seek personal satisfaction and challenge, the contribution they will make is far superior to any you could demand of them. It's a brave environment and the result is that there is nowhere to hide in Semco – if you don't do your job well, you won't be included on someone's team requirements for the next six months.

In addition, there is one cardinal rule that forms the bedrock of Semco culture: 'ask why, and always ask it three times'. Like an incessant child seeking answers, Semler believes 'asking why' crystallises thinking and removes default, pat responses, thereby forcing people to appraise the situation properly. If the idea still stacks up after you've asked 'why' three times, move ahead; if not, don't.

Although an unusual example, there can be no doubt that Ricardo Semler displays the hallmarks of leadership excellence defined by Sun Tzu.

————— YOUR THOUGHTS —————

CONTROL THE GAME

Discipline is the bridge between
goals and accomplishment.
- JIM ROHN, Author

The entrepreneurial ideal of business may shun discipline, preferring instead to adhere to the creative laissez-faire approach. Yet, it is quite clear that success is rarely the result of a fortuitous accident but rather the result of consistent, disciplined effort.

Hailed as one of the greatest leaders of the twentieth century, Jack Welch increased General Electric's market capitalisation by over $400 billion during his twenty years as chairman and CEO. His innovative management strategies and leadership style won both friends and enemies but he undoubtedly demonstrated the discipline Master Sun refers to.

During the early 1980s, he was dubbed 'Neutron Jack'. Like the neutron bomb, he was able to eliminate employees without destroying the building. He implemented a controversial forced ranking system that divided employees into three distinct groups, the top 20% of performers, the middle 70% and the bottom 10%. Known unsurprisingly as GE's 20-70-10 system, this disciplined approach to performance management worked. The top 20% were loved and rewarded with

---

FOOD FOR THOUGHT

Ask all your managers one question: 'If we lost our biggest account tomorrow, how would you reduce your expenses by 10% without losing any of your staff?' Have them each write a one-page report and submit it to you. Implement the best suggestions. Have them repeat the process but this time they must consider who they would terminate in a crisis. Do your managers know who the poor performers are? If they do, what are they doing about them now?

bonuses and stock options, the middle 70% were told how they could get into the top 20% and what they could expect if they did and the bottom 10% were managed out.

Welch believes that people need to know where they stand and that failing to differentiate between performance is the cruellest form of management. He is adamant that you need to apply the same rigour to evaluating your people that you do to evaluating your financial statements. Before Welch took over as head of General Electric, stock options were only relevant to senior executives, but he expanded eligibility to include nearly one-third of all employees. The message was loud and clear: do well and we all prosper, do badly and you're out.

Welch was also praised for dismantling the nine-layer management hierarchy, liberating the chain of command that he felt was stifling the business. The simplification of the bureaucracy led to greater efficiencies and allowed a new level of creativity and informality to flourish. Welch's control of expenditure was also ruthless. He reduced inventory, sold off under-performing businesses and between 1980 and 1985, he reduced payroll by 112,000 people. Making a profit is not just about sales, it's about keeping disciplined control of expenses and staying on top of performance.

As Sun Tzu says, '*The consummate leader cultivates the moral law, and strictly adheres to method and discipline; thus it is in his power to control success.*'

YOUR THOUGHTS

RUN WITH THE *5* OPPORTUNITIES

Chance favours the prepared mind.
- LOUIS PASTEUR

Flexibility is as necessary in business as in war, and although planning is imperative, a shrewd business person will always remain open to opportunities that could not have been foreseen in the planning phase. Sticking doggedly to a plan and refusing to adapt to favourable circumstances is foolish.

In the 1990s, Tommy Hilfiger's move from small niche brand aimed at the 'preppy' upper-income US consumer to a global urban fashion icon was more accident than design. For reasons unknown, the Hilfiger logo was embraced by the hip-hop community and it started to appear on rap music videos. Whatever may be said about Hilfiger the designer, no one can dispute his marketing prowess. He seized on the opportunity and started to deliberately design for that market, emphasising the logo and making the baggy even baggier. He recognised the power that urban black fashion had on mainstream America and sought out upcoming rap stars that exuded the street cool that would then be imitated by hoards of suburban kids. In March 1994, Snoop Dogg appeared on *Saturday Night Live* wearing a red, white and blue Hilfiger shirt and Tommy was officially cool.

FOOD FOR THOUGHT

Tell your staff the story of Tommy Hilfiger and Wrigley to illustrate how businesses can change to meet opportunities. Ask your customer services team to actively request and record any ideas or suggestions that they receive in the course of their customer communications. Consciously listening to what your customers are telling you can provide a lucrative source of income if you implement their suggestions. Be sure to reward both the member of your team and the customer if an idea turns out to be useful.

It would have been easy to stick to the existing strategy or dismiss the interest in his brand by the hip-hop community as nothing more than a fad – after all, this market was not huge. But Hilfiger did neither; instead, he recognised the growing influence of rap music and how that would translate into consumer behaviour.

Mr Wrigley – of the chewing gum fame – was also very good at following where advantage led. A born salesman, William Wrigley dreamed of starting his own business. He moved to Chicago aged twenty-nine with $32 to his name and started his entrepreneurial career selling soap. He was one of the first to understand the power of incentive. To make his product more appealing than his competitors, he offered free baking powder with every purchase. The baking powder proved more successful than the soap and he moved his business into baking powder. Again he promoted his product with an incentive, this time two packs of chewing gum. And again the incentive proved more popular than the original product – and the rest is history.

Both Hilfiger and Wrigley were willing to deviate from the plan when a fortuitous opportunity presented itself and exploit it to the max. Their adaptability made them both very rich men.

YOUR THOUGHTS

LEARN TO DECEIVE YOUR AUDIENCE

*We simply assume that the way we see things is the
way they really are, or the way they should be. And our
attitudes and behaviours grow out of these assumptions.*
- STEPHEN COVEY, Author

Learning how to control perception may be important on the battlefield but it's essential in business. Big business spends millions manipulating the public perception of their brand. And small business should spend as much as possible projecting an image of professionalism and sustainability. One of the biggest mistakes small business makes is producing marketing materials that look more like something their eleven-year-old niece would do than the professional face of a thriving business.

Edward L. Bernays mastered the art of spin before there was even a term for it. He honed his craft working in propaganda during WWI. Bernays went on to start the first public relations firm in America in 1919 and reputedly still consulted with clients beyond his 100th birthday.

He was asked by American Tobacco Company to come up with a campaign that would encourage more women to smoke, which he did very successfully. His promotion was, 'Reach for a Lucky instead of a sweet' – implying that smoking would keep you slim. Sales of Lucky increased threefold in twelve months. However, the real challenge was

---

FOOD FOR THOUGHT

Pick up the phone right now and call your business pretending to be a customer. How are you treated? If you are going to adequately manage other people's perception of your organisation, you need to know what that perception is. This is not an exercise to catch people out but to find areas of improvement that could be implemented across the business.

WORDS OF WISDOM

Sun Tzu stated, 'All warfare is based on deception'. What he means by this seemingly devious statement is that the leader's role is to manipulate and manoeuvre the enemy to his own advantage – 'When able to attack we must seem unable'. Perception is more powerful than fact.

that smoking for women was still taboo. In response to this, Bernays took up arms declaring it an emancipation issue. He organised a march down Fifth Avenue with women brandishing their 'torches of freedom'. Rules were changed as a result and, needless to say, American Tobacco Company was delighted with the results.

Granted, Bernays wouldn't get away with that now – blatant lying is no longer allowed in advertising (although, as we'll see in idea 35, it still happens). Remember, too, that this was a time when smoking was not considered harmful. Hopefully, had he been aware of the damage that smoking does cause, he would not have manipulated his audience quite so brilliantly.

Master Sun has advocated the manipulation of enemy psychology to gain advantage. In business, it's imperative that your customers believe in you. Everything you do and say, from how you answer the phone to the quality of your website, builds a picture of your ability. That picture needs to be manoeuvred wherever necessary so as to ensure you get the business. You still need to be able to deliver on that trust, otherwise the manipulation is pointless, but projecting the right image to the marketplace is the crucial first step to business success. And if that requires deception, so be it.

YOUR THOUGHTS

BAIT THE TRAP

If it ain't broke, don't fix it.
- WISE WORDS OFTEN IGNORED

In a competitive business environment, there is a constant battle for market share and brand dominance. And occasionally, even large competitors make very public errors. The rivalry between Pepsi Cola and Coca-Cola is almost as old as time itself. Pepsi have always been No. 2 but they certainly rocked the boat when they introduced the 'Pepsi Challenge' – blind tasting to see if consumers could tell the two brands apart. Much to the horror of Coca-Cola's senior executives, most participants preferred Pepsi's sweeter product. The bait was set.

In the 1980s, Pepsi continued their assault by not only taking the Pepsi Challenge global but also further strengthening their position with the help of celebrity endorsements aimed at the younger end of the market. Coca-Cola were losing ground not only to Pepsi but also to other drinks in the market.

The problem as far as Coca-Cola was concerned came down to taste – the Pepsi Challenge highlighted that time and time again – so Coke took what could be seen as a logical next step… they tinkered with the recipe.

FOOD FOR THOUGHT

Take a look at your primary product or service. Do you know what its USP is? To avoid making a Coca-Cola type mistake, it's important that you understand what makes you different and why your product or service is bought consistently. If you don't know, find out who your top ten customers are in terms of longevity and revenue. Call them and ask why they continue to buy from you. Ask them if there are any circumstances under which they would go elsewhere. Take action on what you discover.

─── WORDS OF WISDOM ───

Sun Tzu talks repeatedly about baiting the trap to defeat the opposition. He says, *'Hold out baits to entice the enemy. Feign disorder, and crush him'*. This idea of baiting the enemy is strongly connected to the issue of deception and is an important part of *The Art of War*.

What Pepsi had succeeded in doing was to bait Coca-Cola into competing on the one issue they wouldn't win. Coca-Cola started work on a new formula and on 23 April 1985, 'New Coke' was launched. A few days later, production of the original Coca-Cola stopped. This two-pronged decision has since been referred to as the biggest marketing blunder of all time. Consumers demonstrated their outrage by boycotting New Coke. Even Pepsi realised the magnitude of the error before Coke did and exploited the situation. They ran a TV advert featuring an old man sitting on a park bench looking devastated, staring at his can of coke, *'They changed my Coke; I can't believe it!'*

Coca-Cola seriously underestimated the power of their brand. Coke, it seemed, had a passionate, loyal and committed market that didn't care whether Pepsi tasted better or not – they would never switch. On 11 July 1985, Coca-Cola chairman, Roberto Goizueta, announced at a press conference, *'We have heard you!'* New Coke was scrapped. The reinstatement of the original recipe was considered so significant that it appeared in a newsflash on ABC News and other US networks and has not been touched since.

Coca-Cola was baited into fighting a battle it never even needed to enter. It was, after all, 'the real thing'.

─── YOUR THOUGHTS ───

DO THE MATHS

*Never neglect details. When everyone's mind is dulled or
distracted, the leader must be doubly vigilant.
- COLIN POWELL*

If Sun Tzu could have peered into the planning room of Hoover
senior executives on the brink of their new 'Free Flights' advertising
campaign, he would perhaps have warned them to slow down and
crunch some more numbers. The urgency of the drive to clear old
stock was sufficient to cloud their forecasting calculations and led to
serious trouble.

There are very few brands whose clout in the marketplace is so
significant that their brand name has become synonymous with the
activity the product is used for. For example, instead of talking about
'vacuuming the carpet' people commonly refer to 'doing the hoovering'.

Yet this global giant launched a marketing initiative promoting two
free return European flights for customers who bought £100-worth of
Hoover products. Bearing in mind this was way before discount airlines
could whisk you off to the sun for the same price as a gourmet sandwich
and a cup of coffee, £100 for two flights to Europe was an astonishingly
attractive offer. Needless to say, the response was massive. Excited by

---

FOOD FOR THOUGHT

Make it standard practice in your business to challenge all marketing
assumptions prior to the launch of any new initiative, especially a
promotional offer involving a third party. Always forecast for both failure
and success. Organisations are often so focused on break-even or what
they'll lose if the campaign doesn't work that they fail to consider the
cost of a runaway success. Sky high response rates can be as devastating
as poor results.

the initial enthusiasm and seemingly undeterred by the implications, Hoover exacerbated the mounting problem by extending the promotion to the USA. Two free return flights to Europe was attractive; two free return flights to the USA was irresistible – the promotion went ballistic! It isn't clear whether Hoover did the right calculations before launch; it can only be assumed that their projected take-up rate was pitifully underestimated, rendering their forecasts invalid.

The campaign resulted in a court case brought by disgruntled consumers that dragged on for four years. The whole sorry episode ended up costing Hoover £50 million and is widely cited as one of the worst ever corporate blunders. To compound the lamentable forecasting for the campaign, Hoover did not have the infrastructure to deal with the demand it generated. The UK division responsible for the promotion didn't survive and was sold to Italian manufacturer, Candy.

Planning is never seen as the sexy side of business but it's certainly a passion killer of profits if you mess it up. Before you implement any strategy, you need to plan for the worst (and best) case scenario to ensure you have the cash and infrastructure to cope.

There is a fine balance between taking measured risks to further the business and weakening the business enough to leave it vulnerable. The wise general wins by doing proper calculations before battle.

——— YOUR THOUGHTS ———

ACT FAST

Do it now and do it proper.
- GREG NORMAN

In business, the same is true. Taking swift action avoids the twin pitfalls of expense and exhaustion. The only people to benefit from delay are the lawyers!

In 1982, a psychopath put cyanide into some Tylenol capsules. As one of the US's most trusted headache products, the results were disastrous – several people died. In response Johnson & Johnson withdrew the entire inventory from the shelves of American stores. A total of 31 million bottles were returned, costing the company a staggering $100 million and their market share plummeted to 7%. The company accepted responsibility even though the crisis was caused through no fault of their own. Their response was swift and candid and they cooperated fully with police and the media from the start.

Johnson & Johnson's Irish-American CEO, Jim Burke, personally appeared on TV to keep people informed. He emerged as an honest, straightforward executive who demonstrated the *Moral Law* discussed in idea 1. Johnson & Johnson's swift action and ethical behaviour saw sales recover quickly and trust in the brand was amplified.

FOOD FOR THOUGHT

Have a look at your things-to-do list and choose an item that has been on there for at least a month. What's holding progress up? Dedicate the rest of today to resolving the issue. Meet with whoever you need to meet; delegate whatever you need to delegate. Whatever you discover, take action and do it now. You may even find the issue is no longer relevant.

Master Sun warns against the damage to morale and resources caused by protracted campaigns. He advocates speed: *'Though we have heard of stupid haste in war, cleverness has never been seen associated with long delays'.*

Four years later, Gerber, the German baby food manufacturer, remained silent when shards of glass were found in their jars of baby food. A similar thing had happened two years earlier and Gerber recalled half a million jars of the affected products. But this time, they made no public comment and didn't recall a single jar. Perhaps they considered the cost and felt it a risk they were prepared to take second time around. However, the media had a field day. Food tampering is never good but it's especially upsetting to consumers when it affects babies. Over 200 reported incidents were not enough to illicit a reaction from Gerber. The only action they did take was to sue the state of Maryland for banning the sale of certain Gerber products.

Unlike Johnson & Johnson, Gerber did not appreciate that brands are built on trust and whose fault the contamination was didn't make any difference to the consumer. What mattered was that Gerber refused to take action and stuck their head in the sand.

There are times in business when nothing but action will suffice and in those moments, delays are never wise. Long battles only serve to weaken your position and make you vulnerable to competitor attack. Stand in the shoes of your customer and do the right thing – and do it fast! As Sun Tzu reminds us, *'Let your great object be victory, not lengthy campaigns'.*

YOUR THOUGHTS

INTEGRATION IS ESSENTIAL

There are three ways of dealing with difference: domination, compromise and integration. By domination, only one side gets what it wants; by compromise, neither side gets what it wants; by integration, we find a way by which both sides can get what they wish.
- MARY PARKER FOLLETT, Social Worker and Author

Integration is an issue for business, whether it's new people joining a team or organisations merging through acquisition or takeover. Often in the rush to fill a position or do the deal, no one is focused on what happens next.

When Franklin Covey was created in 1997 through the merger of Stephen Covey's self-help empire with time-management guru Hyrum Smith, the new organisation made some crucial integration mistakes. As a business training and professional development company, perhaps they, more than most, should have known better. The businesses maintained separate headquarters and people essentially continued to do what they had always done, only now in a spirit of 'them versus us'. The lack of integration and assimilation between the businesses resulted in an increase in overhead costs.

When Maurice and Charles Saatchi started their famous advertising agency, they took the business by storm. Ruffling feathers right from the start, they refused to join the British Advertising Association that

---

FOOD FOR THOUGHT

If you are employing a new person, assign a 'buddy' to them. Whoever's idea it was to employ someone new should be charged with integrating that person into the business. If departments are merging, then several individuals should be allocated integration responsibilities to ensure synergies are realised and barriers broken down.

promoted 'ethical' advertising and openly poached clients. Starting with nine employees in a small Soho office, Saatchi & Saatchi won award after award. Their drive to be No. 1 soon overtook their creativity and innovation and they moved into acquisition – on a major scale.

A ten-year buying frenzy saw them acquire thirty-seven companies to become the largest ad agency in the world. With annual billing of $7.5 billion, distributed through 500 offices in 65 countries, Saatchi & Saatchi had established a truly global presence. But there seemed to be little thought applied to what happened after the deal was done. The people within the businesses that were bought often never even met the brothers, and no attempt was made to incorporate the new business into a standard operating methodology or infuse the Saatchi culture. The acquisitions also brought conflict of interest problems and they lost the Colgate-Palmolive account as a result. Buying businesses was no doubt a lot more exciting than working out how best to harness those new resources in a mutually beneficial way. The signed contract was the start of the process, not the end.

Sun Tzu talks of 'using the conquered foe to augment one's own strength', yet without proper integration into the organisation the new business, new employee or new division can soon become a liability.

YOUR THOUGHTS

PICK YOUR BATTLES

Pick battles big enough to matter, small enough to win.
- JONATHAN KOZOL, Writer and Activist

Helen Steel and Dave Morris would stand outside their local golden arches happily dishing out a London Greenpeace pamphlet called *What's wrong with McDonald's*. In 1990, four years after the offending leaflet was first published, McDonald's sought legal action against Steel and Morris and three other activists. While the others backed down and apologised, Steel and Morris saw an opportunity to get their views heard by a much larger audience than their local Maccers and chose to fight.

The McLibel trial turned into the longest in English history, with an incredible 313 days in court, over seven years. One hundred and eighty witnesses were called to the stand and McDonald's were hauled over the coals for everything from food poisoning charges to staff pay and conditions to bogus recycling claims. They were even accused of infiltrating the ranks of London Greenpeace.

Considering the offending brochure was quite obviously written from a meat-is-murder vegetarian perspective, it is questionable how much notice those emerging from the North London restaurant after wolfing down their Big Mac really cared about the issues being raised. It may be

---
FOOD FOR THOUGHT

Next time you're going into a senior management meeting, write the words McLibel on a Post-it and stick it on the front of your notes. As a manager, you must know your vision and only enter battles that relate to your desired outcome. An obsessive need for control can cloud judgement and dampen spirits. Give your people room to innovate; they will be far more valuable if you do. Choose the battles you get involved in and let the rest slip past.

a valid point of view to those presenting it but it's a minority view that barely warranted a full-on assault by a corporate giant.

What surely started off as a fly in the McDonald's ointment turned into the ultimate David and Goliath battle. McDonald's came across as the corporate bully. Here was a company with thousands of restaurants located across the globe catering for forty million people every day picking on two little veggies from London. Catapulted from relative obscurity to front page news, the original leaflet became a cult collector's item with more than three million copies in circulation in the UK. The internet proved lethal in disseminating information, with countless websites dedicated to following proceedings and unravelling what was becoming a legally complex case. Books and TV documentaries only served to rub salt into McDonald's wounds.

In June 1997, McDonald's were able to claim victory, albeit a hollow one, when Steel and Morris were ordered to pay damages of £60,000. This case serves as a costly reminder about the importance of discernment when it comes to choosing your battles. It is also a pivotal case in terms of demonstrating the power of the internet in levelling the playing field. Corporate misbehaviour can turn from inside story to viral email in a heart beat.

YOUR THOUGHTS

REMOVE EMOTION FROM STRATEGY

I do get angry sometimes, but if I let that feeling take over
it would only cloud my thinking and disable me from making
the right decision when it counts the most.
- LONNIE EARL JOHNSON, Death Row Inmate

Emotion is human. Business is a collection of humans so to remove emotion is all but impossible. And, as we'll discuss in idea 43, emotion is an important part of business success. However, there is a fine line between being human and being stupid.

Wang Computers were a hugely successful manufacturer of word processors in the 1970s. With a PhD from Harvard, Dr An Wang had not only built a $2 billion company from scratch, he also owned several patents in his own name. One of those patents was for a product that was later sold to IBM after four years of arduous negotiations. The result was an intense loathing for IBM which became his blind spot.

Wang was an inventor not a businessman. He developed some innovative products but made a few poor decisions. When his son Fred pointed out that IBM's PC was a serious threat to their word processor, he replied, *'The PC is the stupidest thing I've ever heard of'*. When he eventually did develop a competing product, it was too late to market and used a non-IBM compatible proprietary system. His hatred of IBM,

---

FOOD FOR THOUGHT

Next time you or any of your team becomes emotional, return to the facts. Often emotion enters the decision-making process when the absence of facts has led to assumptions being made. Go back a step and review what you know to be true and what you don't know. Only move forward with discussions when all the unknowns are answered.

> ――――――――― WORDS OF WISDOM ―――――――――
>
> Sun Tzu warns of the leadership dangers posed by inappropriate emotion, 'The general, unable to control his irritation, will launch his men to the assault like swarming ants'. If men are sent to war based on irritation or ego instead of solid strategy, the leader has failed.

who Wang believed cheated him in the earlier deal, was such that he refused to accept what was happening in the market. He let emotion and obsession dictate his strategy and lost out as a result.

When Compaq Computers announced it would open 100 franchised stores across Australia to combat the Dell direct-sell competition, Gerry Harvey was livid. At the time, his stores, Harvey Norman, were selling $97 million-worth of Compaq products across Australia and now they were going into direct competition with him. While the US-based company tried to calm him down and offered a string of incentives to cushion the blow, Harvey Norman would have none of it and terminated the contract. Because computer sales dropped as a percentage of revenue, it's impossible to say how much the business lost in sales as a result of the decision. However, Harvey Norman is a major Australian retailer and Gerry Harvey obviously felt the principle was important enough and that the company strong enough to weather any losses. The move certainly sent clear signals to his other suppliers not to try anything similar.

Master Sun warns that emotion alone is a dangerous catalyst for decisions and must always be tempered with facts to ensure sound strategy directs business, not ego and irritation.

> ――――――――― YOUR THOUGHTS ―――――――――
>
>
>
>
>

SIZE DOES MATTER

*Differentiate your products, provide great service and don't
even think about trying to compete with Wal-Mart on price.'
- MICHAEL BERGDAHL, Business Consultant*

In matters of war, the strength of numbers is obvious. In business, size also has its advantages in terms of resources and sustainability. Corporate history is littered with the carcasses of small businesses spat out by big rivals. Yet thankfully there are enough examples of entrepreneurs willing to take on the big guns to give hope to generations to come.

Take for example the story of Häagen-Dazs ice-cream. As a widowed Polish immigrant, Reuben Mattus' mother sold home-made fruit ice and ice cream pops from a horse-drawn wagon in the bustling streets of the Bronx. As a nineteen-year-old, Reuben followed where his mother left off and in 1932 he started Senator Frozen products. His ices were distributed through drug and grocery stores and he built a successful business. Soon supermarkets were springing up all over America and with their superior refrigeration facilities and convenience, Mattus saw a way for his products to be sold all year round. His most popular product was an ice cream called Ciro's. Unfortunately, Mattus was not the only one to recognise that ice cream was no longer a seasonal

---

FOOD FOR THOUGHT

Consider your top products or services and note who your largest competitor is for each. Write down what advantages you have over them and what advantages they have over you. Particularly focus on technology and speed of delivery. If these are to be the new weapons of business, you need to be anticipating how technology could influence your business and get you ahead of your competition – regardless of their size.

product and the big dairy companies moved into his market. With greater distribution networks, larger production capacity and increased negotiating muscle they soon squeezed Ciro's out of the market. Size, it seemed, did matter.

But thankfully for ice cream aficionados everywhere, Mattus was a determined character committed to making ice cream of superior quality. Undeterred, he turned his attention to creating a luxury ice cream using only fresh cream, real fruit and natural ingredients. In a twist of marketing genius, he decided to give his product a Scandinavian-sounding name and Häagen-Dazs was born.

The idea that the large will always defeat the small is still often accurate; certainly the larger businesses have more money and resources to survive a struggle than do smaller concerns. However, with the advent of the internet, this idea perhaps more than any is outdated when it comes to business. It's now possible to go head-to-head with big business and win. Global markets have opened up through technology and it is speed and willingness to embrace that technology that will set businesses apart.

As Rupert Murdoch – a man that knows a thing or two about business – says, *'The world is changing very fast. Big will not beat small anymore. It will be the fast beating the slow.'*

───── YOUR THOUGHTS ─────

ENSURE YOUR 'BIG PICTURE' IS POSSIBLE

The belief that one's own view of reality is the only reality
is the most dangerous of all delusions.
- PAUL WATZLAWICK, Theoretician

In a business context, this can relate to board members, or in some cases senior executives, who drive big-picture strategy without having a grasp on the day-to-day operations of the organisation. With the focus on the goal, no one thinks to check whether it's possible on the ground. Requests for detail are waved off for another time in the excitement of moving forward with the grand plan.

Take Quaker, for example. In 1994, Quaker bought Snapple, a quirky soft drink company. The plan was simple: to repeat the extraordinary success of Gatorade. It was, after all, just another drink – how hard could it be?! Although Snapple's sales had dipped, Quaker believed they could make an impact and jumped in. What they didn't understand, however, was that Snapple's success was largely due to its extensive and dependable network of independent distributors who prepared, bottled, warehoused and sold its product in small shops and petrol stations.

Senior executives focused only on the similarities of the product and not on the differences of either the brand or the business. They were so sure they could repeat what worked before that they didn't pay

---

FOOD FOR THOUGHT

Sometimes it's useful to have a pessimist on the team, someone who will raise the objections and find the problems. If you are planning any changes in your business, make sure that you involve people who will be directly affected by those changes. Find out if your strategy is physically possible with the existing resources and whether those changes are something the customers actually want. Don't assume anything.

WORDS OF WISDOM

Master Sun states that a ruler can bring misfortune upon his army '... *by commanding the army to advance or to retreat, being ignorant of the fact that it cannot obey'*. Mistakes will be made if orders are issued from the safety of court without experience of the combat situation.

---

enough attention to the detail. Quaker set about to change things and tried to make alterations in their distribution policies that weren't even contractually allowable. No one had checked to make sure that the big picture of exploiting the synergies was even possible. Three short years later, Quaker sold the business to Triarc for $1.4 billion less than they paid for it.

Quaker made two of the wrong moves that Master Sun warns against. First, it took what worked in a previous situation and applied the same strategy to a new set of circumstances without taking the time to understand the unique characteristics of the new business. Second, that oversight resulted in senior executives being charged with making changes that were impossible within the business structure.

It doesn't only happen with mergers and takeovers – reinventions and operational overhauls can wreak havoc on an unsuspecting workforce, not to mention customers and suppliers. If the people at the top are too far away from the coal-face of business operations, they can lose touch with what is actually possible.

It's important to aim high and dream big dreams but unless you involve people that really know the capabilities and possibilities of the current team and resources, then you're headed for trouble.

YOUR THOUGHTS

_____

_____

_____

_____

EMPLOY THE RIGHT PEOPLE FOR THE JOB

There are only three rules of sound administration:
pick good men, tell them not to cut corners, and back them to the
limit. Picking good men is the most important.'
- ADLAI STEVENSON, Politician

Finding the right people for the job – especially in senior roles – is imperative for business success. The problem is that often the characteristics that made someone excel in their career and put them in line for leadership may not be the same characteristics that are needed to move the business forward. Look at Dr Wang in idea 12 – he was a brilliant innovator and gifted technician but a lousy businessman and his business paid the price.

When Michael Miles was appointed chairman and CEO of a US tobacco giant, it probably raised a few eyebrows. For a start, Miles was a non-smoker. All of his experience was in the food side of Philip Morris' empire, which in the year of his appointment enjoyed revenue of $61 billion. Marlboro and other branded cigarettes were struggling against the unbranded cheaper products on the market, including some made by Philip Morris. In an effort to stem that tide, Miles slashed the price by 25% in a move that would become known as *Marlboro Friday*. The company's share price plummeted by 23% in one day. Essentially, he did not have experience in the tobacco sector and, as he didn't even

---

FOOD FOR THOUGHT

If you have a position to fill, work backwards not forwards. Imagine you're three months down the track having hired the perfect person for the job. What is that person doing on a daily basis? Who are they managing? What solutions and skills do they bring? Use that information to construct a job description and find *that* person.

smoke, he didn't understand his customers or what Marlboro stood for. Just over a year later, Miles resigned. Ironically, his strategy did eventually work but his lack of understanding combined with his aloof and uncommunicative style didn't win him many allies and his position became untenable.

Or what about Boo.com? The concept was quite simple – create an e-tailing business where customers could buy hip and funky sportswear online. Ernst Malmsten, one of the Swedish founders, was quoted as referring to Boo.com as 'a gateway to world cool'. Only problem was they hired the wrong people to create the gateway. Creativity is all very well but an internet business needs a technology platform that works. Focusing on innovative front-end design instead of back-end technology resulted in a site that looked fabulous but took a fortnight to load. In the space of eighteen months, the company rattled through $185 million and went from Boo.com to Boo Who?!

Master Sun warns of the dangers of *'employing officers without discernment'* and the damage it can do to morale. Always reverse engineer the position; don't look at who you've got and see if they fit. Find out what's needed and find a match. If you don't, the business will suffer and your employees will revolt.

YOUR THOUGHTS

MAKE NO MISTAKES

He alone is wise who can accommodate himself to all
contingencies of life; but the fool contends,
and struggles like a swimmer against a stream.
- PROVERB

Master Sun's observation that mistakes can be fatal and one should always guard against them isn't rocket science. Certainly, no one sets out to make mistakes. Hindsight is a marvellous locator of error but few people have a crystal ball.

Xerox is often cited as making a huge mistake by not recognising the potential of the 'information processor' they developed that was later adopted by Apple. Steve Jobs of Apple famously said that Xerox 'grabbed defeat from the greatest victory in the computer industry'. That may be true and certainly they did set up a research facility specifically to develop technology that would expand their brand (more on that in idea 28). But Xerox did what countless business schools advise – they stuck to their core competencies (core competencies, incidentally, that had made them extremely successful).

The same can be said for IBM. By the time 'Big Blue' decided to enter the PC market in 1980, Apple had become a $100 million business (having pioneered the desktop computer with the help of Xerox's earlier oversight). Already in catch-up mode, they decided to source

---

FOOD FOR THOUGHT

Instruct your executives to keep an 'anticipation registry'. In this, they should record any insights or observations about how the market is changing. No censoring allowed. It's good to think outside what's currently possible. That way you can be prepared for the future when it arrives or, even better, you and your business can be part of its creation.

Sun Tzu reminds us, 'Making no mistakes is what establishes the certainty of victory, for it means conquering an enemy that is already defeated. Hence the skilful fighter puts himself into a position which makes defeat impossible, and does not miss the moment for defeating the enemy'.

the microprocessor and the operating system externally. Intel and Microsoft stepped up and the rest is history. That said, IBM was a very successful hardware giant and their strategy at the time was making them a lot of money – so why change? As was the case with Xerox, IBM's requirements were not among their core competencies; they had neither the time nor the experience to develop them internally. So perhaps it's unfair to cite either of these as mistakes.

If it's mistakes you're after, then what about the Smith and Wesson mountain bike? The famous US gun manufacturers decided it was time to capitalise on their name. However, someone obviously forgot to tell them the cardinal rule of brand extension – the extension must be related to the core brand. In the wrong hands, they can both kill and they are both made of metal but that's where the similarities end.

Bic's brand extension into disposable underwear was another howler. How a company famous for disposable pens, lighters and razors could think the next big thing was disposable tights is unfathomable. That too was a mistake.

No one plans to make mistakes but Master Sun's point is that you have to close all the loopholes, cover all the bases, cross all the t's and dot the i's. Then, and only then, will you put yourself 'into a position which makes defeat impossible'.

YOUR THOUGHTS

CONTROL THROUGH DIVISION

Think global, act local.
- MANAGEMENT EDICT

The issue of size is a constant concern in business, especially as business grows and expansion causes its own challenges. The optimum size of a company or workgroup is open to debate. Virgin chief Richard Branson believes fifty to sixty is enough – his Virgin businesses are known for their flat structure to ensure everyone has a voice. Tom Peters suggests 150 and Bill Gates thinks that 200 employees is best. No one adheres to thousands. So what happens when big business becomes bigger?

For many companies, the layers of management and stifling bureaucracy creep across the business creating a fog of inertia. It becomes incredibly easy for employees to hide and for productivity and creativity to dwindle. Decisions take an age to action and survival is a product of economies of scale rather than creativity and innovation.

When the Swedish Asea merged with Swiss company Brown Boveri in 1987, a global giant was created. Within hours of the settlement, Asea Brown Boveri (ABB) had bought fifteen companies. Within two years, it had added forty other companies to the business. By 1998, ABB had 213,000 employees working in 150 countries.

FOOD FOR THOUGHT

Take out your organisational chart, if you have one. If you don't have one, draw it on a blank piece of paper. How many layers are there between the very top and the very bottom? If there are more than four, you need to be asking why. If the people that speak to your customers are not in a position to be able to speak to you or management about their experiences, then you're losing valuable intelligence. Seek to either minimise layers of management or incorporate open communication channels.

Percy Barnevik, orchestrator of the merger, recognised the mutual synergies between the two businesses and demonstrated the courage and trust to make it happen. Hailed as the European Jack Welch, Barnevik too hated bureaucracy. In their book *The Dancing Giant,* authors Kevin Barham and Claudia Heimer state, *'The challenge set by Mr Barnevik was to create ... a streamlined, entrepreneurial organization with as few management layers as possible.'*

Barnevik rose to that challenge and introduced a complex matrix structure for *dividing up the numbers.* Known by Gören Lindahl, Barnevik's successor, as 'decentralisation under central conditions', the company is run by executive committees. Under them, the organisation is divided by business area, company, profit centres and country.

Although the company has divested some operations recently, it still operates in 100 countries and is surprisingly successful at keeping this globally connected business together. The aim was simply to harness the power of a large organisation without getting trapped by the size. Small companies have many advantages over their clumsy counterparts – for one, they are much more agile and are able to adapt to changing conditions quicker. Barnevik was keen to ensure those advantages were not lost to ABB and in so doing, he successfully controlled a large force as though it were a few people.

YOUR THOUGHTS

BUILD STRENGTH AND AGILITY THROUGH SYSTEMS

If a better system is thine, impart it;
if not, make use of mine.
- HORACE

If you want to ease the transition from a small business to a large business, then you would be wise to institute policies and procedures – unless, of course, your business doesn't mind losing vast sums of money through the inevitable inefficiencies that creep in when there are no standard protocols.

Weaving systems and procedures into the fabric of an organisation is prudent for businesses of any size. Why have your people reinventing the wheel all the time when there already exists a best way to do what you do. It is this discipline in operations that has made franchising so successful. And what better franchise to illustrate the point than McDonald's.

McDonald's is remarkable for many reasons – how it started, its growth, bad press (*Super Size Me*), lengthy court battles and their recent reinvention. The debate regarding the quality of their food is not one for these pages but what is amazing is that whether you order a Big Mac in Moscow, Delhi or New York, your experience will

---

FOOD FOR THOUGHT

Is there anyone in your business or team whose sudden departure from the role would cause chaos? If there is, you need to make it your mission and part of that person's job specification to get the information out of their head and into written policies and procedures. That way if they win the lottery or are unable to work, your business doesn't suffer. Only by documenting best practice will you ever stand a chance of consistently delivering it.

fundamentally be the same, be that from how your order is taken, processed and delivered to the taste of the finished product. The consistency of experience is made possible by the McDonald's system – a tight set of procedures that franchisees must adhere to.

It's a system that obviously works, with 70% of McDonald's restaurants worldwide owned and operated by independent men and women. The standardised approach means that McDonald's does *'fight with a large army'* – 31,500 restaurants in 118 countries. But they do so through a system that effectively protects their brand and ensures a consistent customer experience. Plus the franchisee doesn't have to worry about how best to make the business work – they just follow the system and reap the rewards (less a fat slice to HQ).

I'm pretty sure the signs and signals that Sun Tzu was talking about have no relationship to franchising but good business is not an accident (if it is, it isn't sustainable). Good business is more often down to the boring, everyday ability to duplicate good performance. Good performance needs systems and procedures that allow that duplication to occur regardless of who turns up for work today. All too often, team leaders and managers are held to ransom by key personnel whose knowledge and experience has never made it out of their heads and on to paper, thus leaving the business vulnerable should something unexpected happen to those people.

YOUR THOUGHTS

BE DECISIVE

Indecision and delays are the parents of failure.
- GEORGE CANNING

In business, there is rarely anything to be gained from sitting on the fence. A leader's job is to make the hard decisions, even when all the facts are inaccessible. Waiting until all the questions are answered can be commercial suicide.

As Chris Galvin rose through the ranks of Motorola, the company founded by his grandfather in 1928, his determination and decisiveness impressed those around him. Unfortunately, according to analysts, those skills deserted him once he took on the role of CEO in 1997. In the fast-moving technology sector, speed and conviction are essential ingredients for success.

Galvin took eighteen months to finalise the sale of its semiconductor component business despite being told by the president of the division that the sale would return the business to profitability.

It was the same with Iridium, a portable phone system that would work anywhere thanks to sixty-six satellites orbiting the globe. The business, given the go-ahead by Galvin's father in 1991, was, some say, fuelled by 'techtosterone' and had already cost Motorola $5 billion plus. Iridium

---

FOOD FOR THOUGHT

Take a decision that you are currently mulling over. Write down the key things that are stopping progress. Of those things, what can you solve right now? What answers do you need? Who do you need to involve to get the information you require? Whether you get the information or not, commit to making a decision by a certain date. Sometimes, a good decision now is better than a perfect decision later.

> **WORDS OF WISDOM**
>
> Master Sun talks of decisions as the *'well-timed swoop of a falcon'*. *'Energy may be likened to the bending of a crossbow; decision, to the releasing of a trigger'*. What he's saying is that once the information has arrived, be decisive and advance with force and commitment from that decision.

didn't catch on. By late 1999, all of his most trusted advisers were telling him to get out. The business had already filed for Chapter 11 bankruptcy protection, yet it took a further year and an estimated $200 million before he did.

Galvin himself denies being indecisive: *'When people bring high quality of thought on a proposal or an investment and all the questions are answered, we make decisions in nanoseconds.'*

Galvin is not the only Motorola CEO to drag his heels. Gary Tooker, Galvin's predecessor, stuck to his analogue guns and missed digital. Initially, there were three competing standards and with no certainty over which one to back, he waited. Motorola had developed the microchip for Apple years earlier and perhaps didn't want to find themselves backing the wrong horse again. Unfortunately for Motorola, however, Nokia and Ericsson didn't wait. By 1998, Motorola's market share in the US had slipped to 34%, down from 60% four years earlier. Their refusal to embrace digital technology quickly enough was a serious mistake.

There is nothing more frustrating than a leader who won't make decisions. Morale is affected and enthusiasm soon gives way to lethargy and frustration.

> **YOUR THOUGHTS**

HARNESS THE POWER OF TEAMS

No problem is insurmountable. With a little courage,
team work and determination a person can overcome anything.
- B. DODGE, Author

If you can pull the team together and unite them in a shared vision, the whole is worth more than the sum of its parts. Your team or workgroup is more productive as a collective than it is as individual units.

In 1983, Springfield Remanufacturing Corporation (SRC) was a struggling business on the brink of bankruptcy. Although inexperienced in running a company, one of the managers, Jack Stack, and twelve of his colleagues raised $100,000 and bought the business in a leveraged buy-out from parent company International Harvester.

The company has since grown from being $10,000 away from closure to a collection of twenty-two separate companies with combined revenue over $120 million. Many of those new businesses have been spawned from company weaknesses identified by employees – employees who, thanks to Jack Stack, now have a vested interest in the corporate objectives.

He may not have fully understood management but Stack understood the rules of competition and democracy and wanted to create a business

---

FOOD FOR THOUGHT

Set your next project up as a game. Bring the workgroup together and collectively assign players, set the ground rules and make sure everyone understands the objective. Define ways to measure progress so that everyone knows whether they are winning or losing. Give the project a timeline and collectively discuss rewards for success and consequences for failure – make them personal. Have fun and try doing business a little differently.

that was about having fun, playing fair, keeping score and having a voice. He wanted people in the business to own the business and for that to galvanise the shared vision. The result was open-book management and it has proved an extremely successful way of harnessing the *combined energy* of a team. An affiliated business, The Great Game of Business, has grown out of the philosophy and Stack now also teaches others how to emulate his results.

Basically, he advocates that a business should be run like a game. Set the rules, keep score, assign players, have fun and share the rewards. Each year, SRC tackles a challenge that is keeping them up at night. The challenge is turned into a company-wide game, where a significant portion of employee compensation is tied to the outcome. Not only are solutions found but the process is also a fun team-building exercise. And it's not all about the short term – everyone in SRC knows how to read a balance sheet, they have access to information and therefore understand what their decisions mean to the bottom line. Stock options and bonuses mean that a large part of the equity in the business is distributed among the people that create it.

Even Master Sun would have been impressed with SRC's collective ability and what can be achieved when you *'pick out the right men and utilise combined energy'*.

———————————— YOUR THOUGHTS ————————————

FIRST-MOVER ADVANTAGE

*If you're attacking your market from multiple positions and
your competition isn't, you have all the advantage and it will
show up in your increased success and income.'*
- JAY ABRAHAM, Marketing Guru

First-mover advantage is often cited as a benefit for business. The best way to become a strong brand is to be first to arrive in a new territory – then dominate it.

Take the humble Post-it, for example. For nine years the weak adhesive developed by Dr Spencer Silver at 3M's central research department sat on the shelf looking for a purpose. Arthur Fry, a new product developer with 3M, sang in his local church choir. He used slips of paper to mark his place but they kept falling out. Hence, he dug out Silver's adhesive and eureka – the Post-it made its debut. After demonstrating them in offices across the country, Post-it's caught on and 3M created a new market. A market they have dominated ever since.

Similarly, Häagen-Dazs, discussed in idea 13, was the first to occupy the luxury ice-cream market and has maintained its eminence despite stiff competition. Too many scoops could well have contributed to the creation of another industry.

Weight Watchers is another example of a business that was fresh to the

---

FOOD FOR THOUGHT

It may be harder to create new markets but it is still possible to achieve first-mover advantage within markets. Look at your top product or service and attempt to make it unique in your marketplace. Could you introduce an extraordinary guarantee, or offer longer warranty? Where can you create a point of difference that will give you kudos in a congested market?

fight, although it wasn't the sort of fight Sun Tzu was thinking of. In 1961, Jean Nidetch was fighting her own battle – the battle of the bulge. After being put on a diet by the obesity clinic at the New York Department of Health, Nidetch sought some moral support. Faced, no doubt, with the unexciting prospect of crackers and grapefruit, she invited a few friends around to her Queens apartment each week and Weight Watchers and the diet industry were born. Today, Weight Watchers hosts over 50,000 meetings each week across thirty countries.

The only place that first-mover advantage doesn't work so well is in the technology sector. Here, consumer behaviour is often way behind technological breakthroughs. Sometimes, the companies themselves are slow to realise the power of the technology at their fingertips. The rapid adoption of SMS messaging, for example, took most European mobile phone companies totally by surprise – so much so that many didn't even explain the facility in their instruction booklets.

Coca-Cola is able to build a following based on a secret recipe. But technology can often be replicated. New technology can be developed or modifications can be made to circumvent patents and it's not long before the competition is nipping at the first mover's heels. Remember Betamax? That said, being first in the field is usually an advantage – and especially so if your product isn't a gadget.

—————— YOUR THOUGHTS ——————

GO WHERE THERE
IS NO COMPETITION

*Innovation is the creation of the new
or the rearranging of the old in a new way.'*
- MICHAEL VANCE, Creative Thinking Guru

In 1979, when the Walkman was launched, portable tape recorders were not new. Sony themselves marketed a similar product called The Pressman to professional journalists. Its main feature allowed reporters to record their interviews and dictate notes.

Honorary chairman Masaru Ibuka used Sony's first attempt to develop a portable tape player to break up the monotony of his frequent air travel. But the device was bulky (and expensive) so he and chairman Akio Morita instructed Kozo Ohsone, head of the tape recording division, to make a smaller version. The Pressman was modified by removing the record function, adding stereo circuits, a headphone terminal and lightweight earphones. The Sony Walkman was born. Since then, over 150 million units have been sold around the world. Sony took an (almost) existing product, tweaked it and launched it with a completely different proposition to a completely different audience. It was no longer a niche tool aimed at professionals but a vital ingredient to youth, freedom and liberation. It offered people something they

---

FOOD FOR THOUGHT

Is there a new market or new product lurking in your current offering? Gather a task force and see if you can identify a new audience who might use your product for a purpose other than the one you intended. Then look at the market you already serve and see if there are any niche areas within that market where you could either modify the product or the selling proposition so as to appeal more directly to them.

WORDS OF WISDOM

Master Sun says, 'An army may march great distances without distress, if it marches through country where the enemy is not. You can be sure of succeeding in your attacks if you only attack places which are undefended. You can ensure the safety of your defence if you only hold positions that cannot be attacked'.

---

never even knew they wanted – music on the move. In so doing, Sony marched far into a market that was not defended.

In 1989, Paul Cave was involved in organising a one-off climb over the arch of Sydney Harbour Bridge as part of an international business convention. It was a great success and Cave wanted to make the experience accessible to everyone. It took him nine exhausting years before the first commercial climb took place. The logistics of turning an international landmark into a commercial tourist activity was tricky – negotiation with dozens of organisations, including state and local government, community groups and hundreds of experts on everything from national heritage and conservation to safety. More than two million people have climbed Sydney Harbour Bridge since 1998 at an average adult price of $230 – you do the numbers!

Again this example illustrates first-mover advantage. It is also one of the rare examples of a business that can't be duplicated. The first mover was also the last mover. If you want to climb one of the world's most iconic bridges, look down on the Sydney Opera House and gaze across the city, then you can only do so with that company. He has therefore ensured the safety of its defence by holding a position 'that cannot be attacked'.

YOUR THOUGHTS

CONCEAL YOUR PLANS

While all deception requires secrecy,
all secrecy is not meant to deceive.
- SISSELA BOK, Philosopher and Ethicist

In a lesson on both speed and secrecy, there can be few better examples than the merger between Sweden's Asea and Switzerland's Brown Boveri mentioned earlier in idea 17. Founded in 1883 and 1891 respectively, the 50:50 merger announced on 10 August 1987 took the corporate world by surprise.

Not only did the merger create a $30 billion giant but it was also done with incredible speed and simplicity. When Percy Barnevik, Asea's CEO, approached Brown Boveri, he no doubt appreciated what Wall Street did not. This was not as they reported afterwards a merger 'born out of necessity not love' but a perfect match. Brown Boveri was international but didn't excel in management. Asea was not international but had strong management.

Brown Boveri was Switzerland's industrial jewel, a 100-year-old company that had built much of the country's infrastructure. Had talk of the merger leaked out, Barnevik was sure the government and union factions would block the move. So instead, he first chose to negotiate

---

FOOD FOR THOUGHT

When you embark on negotiations with anyone, either internally or externally, first assess who could be against the proposal. Write down three advantages and three disadvantages of the proposal and note next to each who is likely to be affected. Who might feel vulnerable and react negatively? If possible, speak with each individual separately and pre-empt their reaction. Find out what would need to happen in order to gain consensus.

with a tiny group of executives from each company. When the boards were shown the subsequent draft agreement for the first time, some directors had no idea that a merger was on the agenda. They were given an hour to read the papers. There was no due diligence and no lawyers; instead, Barnevik read the draft agreement out to the negotiating team line by line. Objections were raised and handled as they progressed through the document. If no one spoke up, it was taken to mean that everyone agreed.

Barnevik reflected afterwards in a 1991 interview with *Harvard Business Review*, *'We had no choice but to do it secretly and to do it quickly … There were no lawyers, no auditors, no environmental investigations, and no due diligence. Sure, we tried to value assets as best we could. But …we were absolutely convinced of the strategic merits.'*

The fact that it was a merger and not a takeover surely helped, as did the willingness of both management teams to trust each other and move forward. Each recognised the fit and the advantages that a joint venture could secure. Lawyers were replaced by trust and shared vision and the then largest cross-border merger was hailed as a great success. By keeping plans secret until the last minute, Barnevik ensured that they were not jeopardised by *'prying spies'* – in this case, the government or the unions.

YOUR THOUGHTS

ONE SIZE DOES NOT FIT ALL

The three great essentials to achieve anything
worthwhile are, first, hard work;
second, stick-to-itiveness; third, common sense.
- THOMAS EDISON

The same can be said for business. While there may be aspects of success that hold true from one business to another, or one product to another, it is a mistake to assume that a success in one market can naturally translate into another. Quaker, discussed in idea 14, made precisely this error by assuming Snapple could be Gatoraded! Assuming all things will remain equal when you alter one element of the business success formula is bound to backfire eventually. Each situation is unique and must be assessed as such. And a little common sense won't hurt either.

Gerber are a very successful baby food manufacturer, known for their pureed fruit and vegetables in small jars with cute little babies on the front. In 1974, however, they attempted to diversify into the adult food market. The theory was sound. Indeed, we've just discussed it in idea 22: look at what you already produce and assess whether you could tap into a new market for that product or service. But it's hard to see

---

FOOD FOR THOUGHT

Regarding what your company currently delivers, ask yourself whether those innovations were initiated 'outside in' or 'inside out'. If genuine outside influences such as customer feedback and legislative changes are at the heart of the amendments, then you're probably on the right track. If on the other hand the developments are based on internal assumptions that are seeking to influence the external market, then you need to verify that through external research.

how anyone in their right mind would have thought the idea of people coming home after a hard day at the office for a jar of 'Creamed Beef' followed by 'Blueberry Delight' was a winner. The marketing disaster was amplified by the fact that Gerber used the same jars for the adult product as they did for the baby range. By maintaining the same tactics, as Susan Casey pointed out in the October 2000 issue of *Business 2.0*, 'they might as well have called it *"I Live Alone and Eat My Meals From a Jar"'*.

A more recent example of a product blooper is Heinz's Funky Fries. Again the logic might have been valid in principle but the execution was plain wrong. If kids already loved the plain fries, they were bound to love cinnamon, chocolate, sour cream or blue-coloured fries – right? Actually, no. Funky Fries were pulled from US shelves after a year of poor sales.

The challenge for many companies is developing new lines without having those new products cannibalise their existing product range. It makes sense to always keep an eye on the future and try to diversify your offering, but you shouldn't assume that what has worked in the past will automatically apply to different segments of the market. You need to assess each situation afresh – and from the consumers' perspective, not your own.

YOUR THOUGHTS

STRATEGIC RIGIDITY IS DANGEROUS

It is not the strongest of the species that survive, nor the
most intelligent, but the one most responsive to change.
- CHARLES DARWIN

Henry Ford was by history's standards an eccentric genius, still to this day attributed with some of the greatest business decisions of all time. As the father of mass production, Ford was an innovator and a shrewd businessman.

In 1914, he decided to increase his workers' pay from $2.50 to $5 a day. It was a decision fuelled perhaps more out of self-interest than employee welfare because he realised the importance of keeping people. Doubling the workers' wages certainly went some way to appease the tedium of working on his production line and staff turnover improved. But perhaps most importantly his decision to increase their pay ensured that his own staff could afford to buy his cars. At the same time, Ford also reduced the working day from nine hours to eight – perhaps so that they had a little extra time to drive it!

His dedication to producing no-frills reliable cars was incredibly successful; at one point, the company had cash reserves of $1 billion. By 1920, Ford was producing one Model T every minute. However, he

---

FOOD FOR THOUGHT

Identify your most and least successful product or service. Taking each in turn, find out when it was last reviewed for relevance to the market. Since inception, look for three ways that the product or the market it serves has changed. Address those issues now. Even a great product runs the risk of becoming obsolete if you do not pay attention to changing customer needs.

also made some mistakes born out of his determination to maintain the status quo.

Ford gave the market what it wanted. As far as he was concerned, he was going to continue to do so – but he didn't appreciate that the market was changing, or at least if he did, he refused to act on it. Meanwhile, over at General Motors, Alfred P. Sloan believed that customers wanted variety. In a marketing first, Sloan split the market into more detailed segments targeting each of his five models – Chevrolet, Oldsmobile, Pontiac, Buick and Cadillac – to particular segments of the car-buying public. Where Ford offered a functional, reliable Model T, GM offered choice.

Another all-American brand that suffered the same fate was Rubbermaid. Its demise from a $1.45 billion-revenue business was largely due to inflexibility in the face of change. Its place in the market was based on innovation not price and, as a result, cost-cutting and operational efficiencies were not high on the agenda. But as technology advanced, competitors quickly copied their new products; their quality rose to meet that of Rubbermaid's, who consequently lost market share. When they eventually did respond to the challenges they faced, it was too late.

Both Ford and Rubbermaid refused to shape their course according to the nature of the market and paid the price.

YOUR THOUGHTS

NEVER BE AFRAID TO ADMIT
WHEN YOU'RE WRONG

*There is a certain degree of satisfaction in having
the courage to admit one's errors. It not only clears up
the air of guilt and defensiveness, but often helps
solve the problem created by the error.*
- DALE CARNEGIE

In idea 7, we looked at the battle between Coca-Cola and Pepsi. Coca-Cola were under attack and their No. I position in the market looked genuinely threatened for the first time.

There was less than 5% separating the two brands when it came to market share. Coca-Cola invested heavily in advertising but with little effect. The success of The Pepsi Challenge encouraged Coca-Cola to look at the issue from the wrong perspective. They chose to enter the battle based on taste and it took them down the wrong path.

Coca-Cola decided that the only thing to do was improve the recipe so as to ensure their ongoing prominence in the market. New Coke was created and despite consistent negative market research about the possibility of changing the famous drink, Coca-Cola launched their new product and simultaneously stopped production of the original.

Consumers made their displeasure felt and refused to buy the new product. Their saving grace, however, was that Coca-Cola realised their

---

FOOD FOR THOUGHT

Think back to the last time you made a mistake. Go on, try harder! Everybody makes mistakes but it takes real strength of character to admit to them. Once you've thought of a situation, pick up the phone and apologise to the people most directly affected. You might be pleasantly surprised by the results.

mistake and did so reasonably early. No one likes to be wrong and certainly when that mistake is so public and so costly, it can't have been easy to back down. But they did; within ninety days they reversed the decision and reinstated 'the real thing' back to a disgruntled customer base.

Despite the huge blunder, Coca-Cola's top management were not fired. On the contrary, CEO Robert Goizueta received $1.7 million in salary and bonuses for his part in the debacle. Ironically, removing original Coke only served to intensify brand loyalty upon its celebrated return. Conspiracy theorists even went so far as to say it was a deliberate marketing ploy. What better way to get people to appreciate your product than by removing it from circulation? Donald Keough, the company's chief operating officer, denied the claim, saying, 'The truth is we are not that dumb, and we are not that smart.'

Their willingness to admit they were wrong went a long way in reversing the initial damage they did to their brand and renewing the bond between Coca-Cola and their customers. In the company's annual report, Goizueta was cited for his 'singular courage, wisdom and commitment in making certain decisions'. Of course, this was no doubt helped by the fact that Coca-Cola stock reached an all-time high at the beginning of 1986. Perhaps if the lost revenue had not been recovered, they might not have been so forgiving.

—————————— YOUR THOUGHTS ——————————

REWARD YOUR PEOPLE

If the frontline people do count, you can't prove it by
examining the reward systems in most organisations.
- KARL ALBRECHT, Entrepreneur

When you plunder a countryside, let the spoil be divided amongst your men; when you capture new territory, cut it up into allotments for the benefit of the soldiery. Interpreters of *The Art of War* might argue this was not what Master Sun meant by this statement. Instead, it refers to the need to use the enemy's resources to augment the battle. However, from both interpretations there are correlations with business. As the business grows into new territories or sales expand in those territories, the business must harness those new resources to take it to the next stage. And distributing those benefits among those involved is a sensible business decision.

Brad Hill started his career as an executive rewards consultant. If you don't know what they do, they design stock-option incentive plans for big business and find innovative ways to help the rich get richer. However, Hill got sick of this and turned his focus on the other end of the employee spectrum. Inspired by his grandfather, who, he explains, never really had 'a sense of purpose, a sense that his work, and his life, were worth something', Hill set out to find ways to help such people get the pay and respect they deserved.

FOOD FOR THOUGHT
If your business does not implement a profit share or reward distribution programme, make it your mission to design one. Ask for volunteers to create a design team and explore ways of creating a self-funding reward scheme. It could be as simple as asking staff to submit improvements or cost-cutting suggestions. Any ideas that are implemented successfully result in the individual responsible being rewarded with a percentage of the change in revenue or a flat fee.

When he was brought in to Premium Standard, a pork-processing plant in Missouri, many of the staff were being paid $10 an hour to perform some pretty undesirable jobs. Needless to say, people don't stay doing horrible jobs for long and 200% staff turnover each year was common in the industry. In each business he entered, Hill formed a 'design team'. After a crash course in the theory and practice of gain-sharing, the volunteer group represented by each department set about creating a new way to measure and reward staff. They were also taught how to juggle as a way to open their minds to the idea that old dogs can still learn new tricks.

The result at Premium Standard was that staff retention rates doubled. The goal is always to create a self-funding compensation plan and that was achieved. One employee-initiated change to production procedures resulted in savings for the company of more than $13,000 a month, and total monthly savings ran as high as $300,000.

Similarly, in an iron foundry in Michigan, absenteeism, production errors and overtime claims reduced. Union grievances declined by over 90% in just six months. The spoils were divided among the employees and they in turn chose to use some of the money they received to help those less fortunate in their community – a win–win for everyone.

——————————————— YOUR THOUGHTS ———————————————

TALK TO EACH OTHER

You can have brilliant ideas, but if you can't get them across,
your ideas won't get you anywhere.
- LEE IACOCCA

Clear communication is of paramount importance in business. Channels must be fostered from the very top to the very bottom and back again if the ability, skills and potential of any business are to be fully realised.

Take Xerox for example. In 1928, Chester Carlson invented the world's first plain paper copier and in so doing, created a new industry. As a result, the business he founded has become a branding success story perhaps only equalled by Hoover. Xerox is synonymous with its original product and Xerox is often used as a verb, particularly in the US.

By 1968, company sales hit $1 billion but they felt stifled by their legacy. It didn't seem to matter what innovation they came up with, people refused to see them as anything other than an office copier company. Their solution was to develop a dedicated research facility and in 1970, they opened the Xerox Palo Alto Research Center (PARC).

Xerox PARC created dozens of killer applications, including the computer mouse, the Ethernet and the graphical interface that Apple

---

FOOD FOR THOUGHT

Opportunities are missed every day for making or saving more money. The people that have these ideas don't tell anyone because they don't know who to speak to or whether they should. Institute monthly 'blue sky' meetings, in which staff down tools for an afternoon, enjoy a beer and brainstorm ideas about how the business could be improved. As Peter Drucker says, 'The really important things are said over cocktails and are never done!'

later adopted for the Mac, as discussed briefly in idea 16. To be fair, Xerox had their fingers burnt in 1975 when they developed Xerox Data Systems, which failed dismally and cost them $85 million. The only significant invention PARC came up with that did make it into the Xerox production line was the laser printer. Why? There are two reasons that I could find. First, the market simply refused to see Xerox outside its defined sector. The second reason was down to communication. The inventors at PARC were speaking to copier people in Xerox and they simply didn't understand each other. No doubt reminded of Xerox Data Systems, they didn't appreciate or want to understand the possibilities presented by the various inventions. There were in effect no personnel elsewhere in Xerox with the knowledge and vision to run with the new innovations. Communication between the two organisations was poor and billion dollar opportunities were lost as a result.

Perhaps it's a lesson about knowing yourself and just staying focused on your niche. Certainly, there was enough money in it and had Xerox not spent millions trying to be something they were not, Canon and IBM wouldn't have made major inroads into Xerox's market. Perhaps it's a reminder about getting the right people or perhaps it's just a lesson to remind us all to communicate a little more often.

--- YOUR THOUGHTS ---

UNITE AS ONE

*Individual commitment to a team effort – that is what makes a
team work, a company work, a society work, a civilization work.
- VINCE LOMBARDI, American Football Coach*

In business, ensuring everyone is on the same page is imperative
if any real progress is to be made. There has to be a unity of
purpose and shared vision if a business is ever to break out of mere
ordinary performance.

One of the challenges that faced Motorola in the late 1990s was
that fiefdoms had built up over the years. Apart from the six main
divisions, there were also dozens of large operating businesses, each
with their own agenda. Each business, some as large as $1 billion
concerns, marched to the beat of their own drum, they had their
own managers, profit and loss accounts, marketing and development.
Often, a measure of autonomy will breed creativity and focus but, in
the case of Motorola, their highly decentralised management system
created two major problems. First, the resultant warring tribes seriously
reduced cooperation between divisions. The second challenge was
that Motorola used division-based incentives to motivate managers.
Each manager was responsible for his or her own profit and loss and
incentives were dished out based on those results. It is this that is often

---

FOOD FOR THOUGHT

When departments argue, it's often because they don't understand the
importance and relevance of each other's role in the business. Sales
get frustrated with despatch for not fulfilling orders quickly enough;
despatch is frustrated with sales because they never complete all the
information properly. Get the groups together and illustrate the process
that each plays in the goal of the business. Better understanding between
'instruments' can help improve the symphony.

partially blamed for Motorola's slow move to digital mobile phones. Motorola's incentive scheme created a short-term disincentive for managers to take on the cost associated with switching from analogue to digital.

The problem is that when everyone is marching to their own beat, it's hard to hear anything constructive. This fact was not lost on Roger Nierenberg, a professional conductor who has created an innovative way of giving organisations a chance to experience what can happen when you get it right.

The Music Paradigm was started in 1995 and uses a symphony orchestra as a metaphor for a dynamic organisation. Executives are seated among members of a live, professional orchestra. Through a series of exercises the executives are able to witness the correlation between conducting an orchestra and managing a business. Just as the conductor must lead the musicians the CEO must lead his business units and teams.

In one session, Nierenberg leads an executive up to the podium and instructs him to listen. He protests, *'But I want to conduct!'* To which a woman seated in the audience shouts, *'See what I have to deal with every day!'* Everyone laughs. The Music Paradigm has assisted many blue chip clients and seems to be a powerful way of bringing a greater awareness to organisations and business units that shared vision and unity really can achieve great things.

---- YOUR THOUGHTS ----

TURN MISFORTUNE INTO GAIN

When fate hands you a lemon, make lemonade.
- DALE CARNEGIE

When Erin Brockovich was involved in a car accident, she was already down on her luck – after two failed marriages, she had three kids and precious little money in the bank. She hired Los Angeles attorney Ed Masry to seek compensation from the negligent driver but lost the case. In desperation, she begged Masry to give her a job. He did and her initial misfortune turned into such staggering gain that Hollywood made a film about her story, starring Julia Roberts.

What makes her story so special is that the gain was not just hers. She got interested in a case involving residents of a small Californian desert town called Hinkley. Mysterious illnesses had affected the residents, who all lived near Pacific Gas & Electric (PG&E). Although she had no experience, she followed the case like a dog after a bone. Masry realised she was on to something and sued. In 1996, PG&E settled for $333 million. Not only was it the highest pollution lawsuit ever settled in US history but it also meant that hundreds of families seriously affected by corporate negligence got the help they deserved.

FOOD FOR THOUGHT

Look at a past 'failure' or wrong choice your business has made and with the benefit of hindsight, reassess it through fresh eyes. Don't quit until you can find something good that happened as a result of it – either for you or someone else. Perhaps you met someone significant, or learnt a very important lesson, or perhaps you were led in a more fulfilling direction. It's never what happens to us that matters, it's what we make those things mean.

WORDS OF WISDOM

Sun Tzu talks about changing conditions and the importance of adapting to whatever shows up. *'If in the midst of difficulties we are always ready to seize an advantage, we may extricate ourselves from misfortune'*. This ability is born out of strong character and allows us to turn *'misfortune into gain'*.

Who could have predicted that a computer crash would create the management guru industry and propel a McKinsey employee to the top of it? John Larson of McKinsey's San Francisco office was due to give a presentation to a client but the computer meltdown meant he couldn't access it. He needed to find something else or someone else to satisfy the client. Tom Peters, one of Larson's colleagues, had spent time the previous year travelling around the world researching international best practice. Perfect! He instructed Peters to pull it together and give it a sexy title. The result was the forerunner to *In Search of Excellence* and Tom Peters was re-cast as a management guru. Now he fills auditoriums the world over and is the author of many books.

Truth is, his research had been gathering dust. He'd presented his findings to the powers that be in McKinsey's in the summer of 1977 but his research remained vague and inconclusive and Peters returned to his normal assignments. If Larson's computer hadn't crashed, who knows if the research would ever have been revisited and crafted into one of the world's most respected management books.

When opportunities arrive – whether through accident, chance or synchronicity – take them. Always seek to find something good from every challenge you face and *'turn misfortune into gain'*.

YOUR THOUGHTS

AVOID THE FIVE FAULTS
OF LEADERSHIP

Form the habit of making decisions when your spirit
is fresh… to let dark moods lead is like choosing
cowards to command armies.
- CHARLES HORTON COOLEY, Sociologist

According to Master Sun, recklessness, cowardice, hasty temper, delicacy of honour and too much sympathy together form the five nemeses of a leader. Individually these aspects are not necessarily fatal, although it depends on the magnitude. Take for example, Nick Leeson and Barings Bank. Slice it whatever way you want to, but Leeson was reckless and it did lead to the destruction of a financial institution. At 233 years old, however, Barings Bank should have known better and for them to imply that its demise was the sole responsibility of one 'rogue trader' perhaps displays the cowardice that Sun Tzu also refers to.

As part of the old guard, Barings needed young blood to wield the new instruments of global finance and Nick Leeson fitted the bill. Leeson demonstrated ability in these complex markets and advanced quickly through the company, eventually being posted to the SIMEX exchange in Singapore where his job was essentially to bet on which direction global markets would move. In his book *The Collapse of Barings*, Stephan Fay states, '*the directors of Barings came to rely on people they hardly knew – like Nick Leeson – to make their fortunes in markets they did not*

FOOD FOR THOUGHT

Take a decision you are in the process of making or one you have just made and assess it from the angle of each of these faults? Has anger, ego or cowardice played a hand in the choice? Is an unwillingness to make the hard decisions diluting your management? If you have been guilty of these faults, rectify the situation immediately. Apologise if you have to!

fully understand, like SIMEX in Singapore'. And make a fortune he did: his operation yielded spectacular returns and at one point accounted for 10% of Barings' entire operating profit. Still in his mid-twenties, the plasterer's son from Watford was hailed a hero – the 'Michael Jordan of trading'. No one thought to question how it was even possible to make $10 million in a week.

In a final bid to recover the escalating losses he'd been hiding, Leeson bet on the Japanese market going up. Unfortunately for him, Mother Nature had other ideas; a gigantic earthquake hit Kobe on 17 January 1995, bringing the city and Barings to its knees. The losses came in at £860 million – too much even for the Queen's bank to withstand. Leeson fled but was later extradited to Singapore where he served six and a half years in prison for fraud. At the same time, his wife left him and he contracted colon cancer. These days he lives a quieter life in Ireland; in 2005, he returned to his working class roots and was appointed manager for Galway United Football Club. As for Barings, it was bought by ING for £1.

Master Sun warns of the dangerous faults born out of inappropriate emotion. Allowing anger, cowardice, arrogance, fear, stupidity or oversensitivity to pollute your decisions is a recipe for disaster.

YOUR THOUGHTS

STAY HUMBLE

Humility leads to strength and not to weakness. It is the highest
form of self-respect to admit mistakes and make amends for them.
- JOHN JAY McCLOY, Lawyer and Presidential Advisor

If it's humble and successful you're after, look no further than Warren Buffett, the Oracle of Omaha. Buffett is a man of simple tastes despite being the second richest man on earth. There are no Ferraris in the garage; he prefers his new Cadillac. His old car – together with the number plate 'THRIFTY' – was auctioned on eBay for charity in 2006. There's no crowing or bluster; the results speak for themselves. If you bought one share in Berkshire Hathaway in 1964, it would have cost you $19.46; on 25 August 2007, that same share was worth $119,850! He invests only in what he understands and believes in putting all his eggs in one basket. Unlike those in idea 34, Buffett only makes money when his investors make money.

At the other end of the spectrum is a business Buffett didn't touch with a barge pole ...

Enron CEO, Jeffrey Skilling, hung up on the only journalist brave enough to question Enron after telling her she was unethical. Bethany McLean still wrote the article – entitled 'Is Enron Overpriced?' – for

---

FOOD FOR THOUGHT

People want to be inspired to get behind a shared vision but they can become disillusioned if there is too much bluster and not enough action. Next time you're chairing a meeting, spend no more than 20% of it inspiring the group and the other 80% discussing the strategy and planning that will increase your preparations for advancement. Never reverse the split or your words will become hollow and meaningless.

Fortune magazine. Chairman Kenneth Lay tried unsuccessfully to get her fired and CFO Andrew Fastow flew to New York to pressure her to back down, insisting Enron was in great shape. Forceful words ahead of a spectacular retreat. Fastow, the man at the centre of the creative accounting that contributed to the company's downfall, earned CFO Magazine's CFO Excellence award a mere two years before the collapse. Chief Executive Magazine also lauded Enron around the same time, a time when Enron was already up to its neck in fraudulent activity.

Eleven out of sixteen Wall Street analysts covering Enron were still recommending the stock as 'buy', or 'strong buy' to investors weeks, even days, before its collapse. Enron went from allegedly enjoying revenue of $100 billion in 2000 to declaring bankruptcy on 2 December a year later. Clearly, McLean was correct to question Enron and it wasn't her that had behaved unethically.

Despite having friends in very high places, Enron was finished. President Bush distanced himself immediately. Two years later, Bush would be taught his own lessons on humility. In response to the insurgents attacking US forces in Iraq, he said, 'My answer is bring 'em on' – a statement he came to regret and publicly apologised for in 2006. Beginning with bluster does indeed show a "supreme lack of intelligence".

YOUR THOUGHTS

STOP THE WHISPERS

When the eyes say one thing, and the tongue another,
a practiced man relies on the language of the first.
- RALPH WALDO EMERSON

Many a disgruntled employee has fiddled as Rome burns. When staff lose faith in their leader, they can and will do almost anything other than what it is they are charged to do. It is essential to look out for signs of dissatisfaction and provide a platform for airing grievances so the business can successfully move on.

In 1999, Carly Fiorina joined Hewlett-Packard as its new chief executive. She was 1) the first outsider ever chosen to run the business and 2) the highest profile female appointment in the US. Of these two facts, the first was her biggest challenge. Sure, her gender would have caused a stir in some quarters but she had proven herself worthy so her ability was not in question.

Before long she ran into the hardest obstacle of all – a sceptical workforce. Managers and employees never openly attacked her plans for change; instead, they just decided among themselves which they would action and which they would ignore. In public forums, Fiorina appeared to win support but it was often only a façade. Managers

---

FOOD FOR THOUGHT

If you suspect that your plans are not being actioned or there is dissent in the ranks, raise the issue in a public forum and suggest that people contact you with concerns. The only rule is that they are not allowed just to complain – they must state their opinion, anonymously if necessary, but must also suggest a constructive solution to the problem. Investigate each suggestion and implement the good ones.

altered targets and shifted timelines to be more 'reasonable'. Needless to say, by the time they had finished, they had completely changed her vision and made what she was trying to achieve impossible. Resistance was subtle and as a result, she often didn't know about it until it was too late. There was no obvious opponent, just a system that didn't like being changed by an outsider. And a female one at that!

She will probably best be remembered for masterminding HP's $20 billion acquisition of arch-rival Compaq Computers. It was a battle she won against fierce opposition from shareholders, including the founders' heirs, employees and customers. Her board was, however, on her side, and bolstered by their approval for the deal, she persevered. The idea was that purchasing Compaq would create access to higher margin services and essentially allow HP products to be sold all the way along the value chain, from computer to printer to ink. The merger went ahead and for a time, she ran one of the largest businesses in the world. But the predicted advantages didn't materialise and the board asked her to step down. It wasn't all bad news, though – she walked away with $21 million severance pay.

Fiorina failed to get enough people on board and stop the whispers of discontent. That, perhaps more than anything, was her undoing.

YOUR THOUGHTS

EXCESSES SPELL TROUBLE

You show me a capitalist, and I'll show you a bloodsucker.
- MALCOLM X

Although it is tricky to find examples of excessive use of punishment in the workplace, there is no end to excessive rewards.

Had it not been for the spate of corporate collapses, including Enron and WorldCom, the failure of Global Crossing, the telecom network, might have made a little more news. When it filed for Chapter 11 bankruptcy protection on 24 January 2002, it almost slipped by unnoticed despite losses of $7 billion. In the run up to the collapse, chairman, Gary Winnick, cashed in $734 million in stock.

As well as sharing high-powered political connections, an alleged penchant for shredding incriminating documentation and having Arthur Andersen on the accounting team, Global Crossing and Enron shared a few more similarities – a fundamental lack of ethical standards. Enron chairman, Kenneth Lay, pushed Enron stock to employees while privately offloading $108 million of his own holdings just weeks before the collapse. Jeffery Skilling stood down as CEO of Enron on 14 August 2001, just three months before it started to hit the headlines. In the previous three years, he'd made $152 million, although this was

---

FOOD FOR THOUGHT

As part of your self-funding profit-sharing scheme (see idea 27), institute a 'random act of kindness fund'. Anyone in your organisation can apply to the fund to do something kind for a colleague or someone in the local community. Perhaps someone is celebrating a wedding anniversary or a workmate is struggling financially. Being able to help others is often more satisfying than meeting selfish desires and it fosters a community spirit in the workplace.

obviously not enough because just over a month after his resignation
he sold 500,000 of his shares, netting him a further $15 million.

In the case of WorldCom, the board authorised loans of $408 million
to CEO Bernie Ebbers, which he didn't pay back. However, after a law-
suit brought by shareholders, he was ordered to go some way towards
doing so.

Part of the problem with excessive rewards seems to stem from
leaders who have not made the distinction between themselves and
the businesses they lead. Tyco CEO, Dennis Kozlowski, for example,
seemed oblivious to the irony of making passionate speeches about the
need for ethical conduct in business while using corporate funds to buy
a little more than office stationery. Tyco funds paid for everything from
a multi-million dollar art collection to a thirteen-room Fifth Avenue
apartment. Kozlowski and former CFO Mark Swartz were indicted on
thirty-eight felony counts for stealing $170 million directly from the
company and a further $430 million in tainted share deals.

All of these are examples of the frequent (and significant) rewards
dished out at the limit of the corporate resources – and all were taken
leaving employees and shareholders to pay the price. Excessive rewards
are the tell-tale signs of dire distress.

YOUR THOUGHTS

NEVER UNDERESTIMATE
YOUR OPPONENT

Beware the wolf in sheep's clothing.
- CAUTIONARY FOLKLORE SAYING

It's not hard to imagine the reaction of GlaxoSmithKline (GSK) staff when they were first contacted about the research findings of two fourteen-year-old New Zealand students. In a science experiment, Pakuranga College students Anna Devathasan and Jenny Suo tested a variety of their favourite fruit juice drinks, including Ribena, for the presence of vitamin C. Ribena, a blackcurrant syrup-based drink with huge annual sales, has long been a favourite of children the world over, their parents no doubt comforted by the claim that 'the blackcurrants in Ribena have four times the vitamin C of oranges'.

Yet, according to results of the science experiment, Ribena contained almost no vitamin C. The students contacted the company to raise their concerns and were fobbed off. Suo said, *'When we got no response [to a letter and e-mail], we telephoned them but they didn't take us seriously because we were just fourteen.'*

Undeterred, the girls took their observations to the Advertising Standards Authority and *Brandpower,* but it was only after a TV consumer affairs programme, *Fair Go*, picked up the story and suggested

---

FOOD FOR THOUGHT

Compose an analysis of your top three competitors. Write down three strengths that set them apart from their rivals – including you – and three weaknesses. Choose the main strength and brainstorm with your management team how you can improve on it and incorporate those improvements into your product or service offering. Choose their primary weakness and discuss ways to exploit it to your own advantage. Can you draw attention to their shortcomings through your marketing message?

WORDS OF WISDOM

Master Sun talks often about deception and, therefore, warns against being deceived by the enemy and underestimating their ability. *'He who exercises no forethought but makes light of his opponents is sure to be captured by them.'* It's important to properly assess your opponent without prejudice or assumption.

they approach the Commerce Commission that things started to happen. The New Zealand Commerce Commission, the country's corporate watchdog, took up the cause and in March 2007, with the girls, now seventeen, watching from the public gallery, GSK were fined $217,500 for breaches of the Fair Trading Act. GSK, the world's second largest food and pharmaceutical company, with worldwide turnover in excess of $61 billion, admitted to fifteen representative charges that it misled consumers by implying Ribena had more nutritional value than it actually did. The Australian division of GSK also admitted responsibility and the television advertising and claims on drink bottles and packets have since been changed to drop the false claims.

It's impossible to know how much the company made on the back of those claims. Certainly, over the course of their advertising history, it is significantly more than the fine handed down in the New Zealand court. However, it's a timely reminder that you should never make light of your opponent – especially if they are right and they can prove it.

The McLibel court case discussed in idea 11 is also an example of a large organisation underestimating an opponent. McDonald's certainly did not bargain for the impact that the internet could have in bolstering opinion against a global brand.

YOUR THOUGHTS

BALANCE REWARD AND PUNISHMENT

Never tell people how to do things. Tell them what to do
and they will surprise you with their ingenuity.
- GENERAL PATTON

If a business leader is too heavy handed and does not first win the respect of the team, they will not follow; or, as Carly Fiorina found out in idea 33, they may only pretend to follow. Conversely, if the leader is adored by his people but refuses to discipline them, the result is equally unproductive. The key is to find a balance between the two.

In idea 4, we discussed Jack Welch. It can be clear from what's written about him that he had no problem with the discipline side of the equation but what about the other side?

Once the dust had settled on GE's slice-and-dice downsizing, the business needed to be rebuilt. Apparently, Professor Kirby Warren of Columbia University asked Welch how he was going to get some of the work out of GE now he'd got so many of the people out. Welch latched on to the 'work out' concept and brought in some academic heavy hitters and business consultants to nut out the practicalities.

The resulting idea was simple. Groups of between 40 to 100 employees from all ranks of GE would come together in informal meetings to

---

FOOD FOR THOUGHT

Take a problem that is currently keeping you up at night and apply the 'work out' principle. Explain the concept to your people. Give them an overview of the situation, the challenges and desired outcome. Then leave the room. Have them present their findings and decide on the spot to reject, accept or request more information. Involve your people – they may be able to see solutions you'd never come up with.

discuss business problems. The boss would start the sessions with a business review, propose an agenda and then leave the room. Aided by facilitators, the employees then broke into groups and attacked separate parts of the problem. At the end of the session, the boss would return to hear the suggestions and was only allowed to accept, reject or request more information. If more information was requested, the boss needed to allocate a team and commit to a deadline for making the final decision.

'Work out' was a relentless, company-wide search for a better way to do everything, and an opportunity for employees to dramatically change their working lives.

Hailed as a huge success, it helped to rebuild the bonds of trust so devastated by GE's restructure. People were given a platform to express their ideas and concerns. They became actively involved in the change and in creating a better environment and a stronger business. The result was that 180,000 fewer people made $5.65 billion more in earnings. *Industry Week* announced in 1999, '*The most acclaimed SOB of the last decade is the most acclaimed CEO of this one.'*

Welch had found the balance between humanity and discipline that Master Sun spoke so highly of 2,500 years ago.

YOUR THOUGHTS

SHOW CONFIDENCE
IN YOUR PEOPLE

What we expect with confidence
becomes our own self-fulfilling prophecy.
- BRIAN TRACY, Author and Speaker

In idea 3, Ricardo Semler was discussed for his exemplary leadership characteristics. Semler has broken just about every business rule in the book and has created an extraordinary business because of that fact, not despite it. One of the fundamental differences is his boundless faith in his staff.

Semler is a rare leader who actually trusts his people and has demonstrated that trust in a way most observers can't even get their head around. Of course, the staff have to produce what's needed but how they do so and where they do so is left to the people involved.

There can be few places in the world where staff are encouraged to 'ramble through their day', where personal challenge and satisfaction are encouraged before the meeting of corporate goals. Yet, far from being professional suicide, there is unquestionable logic behind it. Most people want to feel needed and useful, as though their contribution is valued and their opinions matter. These are basic human needs yet most businesses ask their staff to leave them at the door.

FOOD FOR THOUGHT

Next time you have a project to complete, consider a different approach. Instead of finalising objectives and dishing out tasks to unwilling participants, call a meeting and tell people about Semler and his innovative approach to business. Explain the project and its timeline and objectives. Then ask for questions and volunteers. Allow those people to swap some of their existing tasks with others if necessary and make the rest up as you go along. Discuss what happened.

WORDS OF WISDOM

There are several references in *The Art of War* to the importance of treating the men well. In this instance, Sun Tzu stresses the benefits of trust: *'If a general shows confidence in his men but always insists on his orders being obeyed, the gain will be mutual.'*

Semler understands what so few seem to – people are people, not machines. As such, they have personal preferences and outside interests and responsibilities that are equally if not more important to them than work. Semler has taken the business rhetoric of work/life balance and instituted some initiatives that genuinely address the issue.

Consider Semco's 'retire-a-little' programme, for instance, which addresses the irony of the life cycle – namely that when you are physically active enough to want to climb mountains, run marathons or enjoy your young children you don't have the money or freedom to do it, but by the time you do, you or the kids are too old. Employees can, therefore, buy as much early retirement as they want.

For example, someone may choose to buy every Wednesday back from the company so they can spend more time with their young children. They would receive slightly less income but would have gained more freedom. And it gets better: when you do retire from the business, you receive vouchers equivalent to the number of 'retire-a-little' days you took in your working life. The employee is then free to redeem those vouchers after retirement if they want to, by selling them back to the business. It's brilliant – the retiree makes a little extra money, continues to contribute in a meaningful way and the business retains valuable expertise. Now that really is mutual gain!

YOUR THOUGHTS

INSTIL SOME ORDER

I long to accomplish a great and noble task,
but it is my chief duty to accomplish small tasks
as if they were great and noble.
- HELEN KELLER

When Philip N. Diehl took charge of the US Mint in September 1994, it was the epitome of everything negative about government bureaucracy. Inefficiency and complacency combined to create a slow-moving organisation without authority or direction. The Mint's primary responsibility was to the Federal Reserve System. It needed to ensure that there was an adequate supply of coins in circulation at any one time. Yet, the disorganisation was such that no one actually knew how many coins were in its inventory.

Diehl was brought in to change things and bring a sense of commercial reality to the 201-year-old government agency. His approach was perfectly weighted; he didn't go in guns blazing and there were no bold promises or dire threats. Instead, he made small incremental changes over his six year tenure. His strong yet respectful leadership gave the Mint clear and distinct orders; duties were assigned and performance standards were raised bit-by-bit. For example, when he arrived, only 50% of coin collectors had their orders shipped within eight weeks.

FOOD FOR THOUGHT

Follow the Mint's example. Seek out a problem that your customers really care about in terms of your product offering. It may be the actual product or the service associated with receiving it. Whatever it is, publicly commit to resolving the issue and don't rest until you do. This process automatically shifts the focus back to where it matters most — the customer experience.

Diehl has said that one of the greatest lessons he learnt was that if you identify a problem that customers really care about and publicly commit yourself to fixing it, you can build an incredible sense of confidence both inside and outside the organisation. Under his authority, shipping was reduced to two weeks. The '50 State Quarters Program' was launched to attract a new generation of collectors and revenue soared. As Diehl points out, 'You do big things by doing lots of small things.'

When an organisation has weak or non-existent leadership, employees struggle to find their place and can't see where their contribution matters. As a result, the business is slovenly and disorganised.

That doesn't mean you have to have employees account for every second of their day. Take 3M, for example. In an effort to continue to bring innovative products like the Post-it note to market, the company introduced 'the 15% policy'. This encourages employees to take 15% out of their working week to roam outside their fixed duties in search of creative ideas that could take the business into new areas.

People need to know where they fit and what duties are expected of them, otherwise they will drift and the business will suffer. Temper fixed responsibilities with a freedom to innovate so that your people have the confidence to bring you good ideas when they have them.

YOUR THOUGHTS

REGARD YOUR EMPLOYEES
AS YOUR CHILDREN

Birds of a feather flock together.
- IDIOM

Why is it that we are still impressed and surprised when we read stories of how businesses prosper when they treat their staff well? Companies like Semco and SRC are seen as anomalies and yet basic common sense would confirm their approach as more than valid. You can, after all, catch more flies with honey than vinegar. Yet 'them and us' management is still by far the more popular way of running companies – despite its obvious and significant failings.

Perhaps it really is as simple as treating your soldiers like children. And if they actually are, then that's fine too! Nepotism often gets a bad press but there are very successful businesses that consciously seek to encourage a genuine family atmosphere.

Southwest Airlines is full of real families – married couples, parents, children and siblings. The company can't say exactly how many employees are related but according to the 'Fun Facts' on their website there are 1,133 married couples. Far from nepotism being a problem, they actively encourage employees to recommend family members. Their only rule is that one family member can't be supervised by another.

FOOD FOR THOUGHT
If you have a position to fill in your business, approach your best people and ask for recommendations. Find the employees in your organisation or work group with a winning attitude, who consistently deliver top-rate performance and who show commitment and loyalty to the business. Ask them if they know anyone either in their family or social circle who would be suitable for interview. If you don't have any consistent performers to ask for referrals, then you've got a whole different set of problems.

WORDS OF WISDOM

'Regard your soldiers as your children, and they will follow you into the deepest valleys', says Sun Tzu. 'Look upon them as your own beloved sons, and they will stand by you even unto death.' By treating the soldiers well, they will fight with loyalty and passion.

Then there's Quad/Graphics, the third largest printer in North America, with sales over $2 billion. It probably holds the record for nepotism – over 55% of the workforce is related! Quad/Graphics have obviously found the balance between commercial success, creating an environment people enjoy working in and hiring the right people for the job regardless of who they are related to. They have been named in *Fortune*'s '100 Best Companies to Work For' in both 2006 and 2007. Quad/Graphics have even built a $5 million apartment complex to offer affordable housing to its employees and at the same time give family members a break from each other. Living and working together can create its challenges.

The theory is simple: if mothers or fathers show a strong work ethic and are good at their job, it's highly likely that they will have instilled their offspring with the same values. It is also argued that there is more candour in these environments and people are less likely to sugar-coat the truth. Southwest have even had parents tell them not to hire their children!

Although Sun Tzu was talking metaphorically, the point being made is that people need to be treated well. When they are, they will display loyalty and commitment akin to family bonds.

YOUR THOUGHTS

DON'T BE TOO SOFT

Give them an inch and they'll take a mile.
- IDIOM

In a business context, treating staff well and rewarding performance is simple common sense. Making every effort to avoid 'them and us' management is important and yet there is a fine line between getting the best from your people and being taken advantage of. Someone who seems to have no problem making his *'authority felt'* or of *'quelling disorder'* is Rupert Murdoch.

Murdoch inherited the *Adelaide News* and *Sunday Mail* from his father in 1952, but he had much greater ambitions than his father. In 1964, he created *The Australian* and promised 'to report the nation to Canberra and Canberra to the nation'. By the end of 1960s, Murdoch had strengthened his Australian position and was looking further afield, firstly to the UK.

As discussed in idea 46, he bought the *News of the World*. He then bought *The Sun* in 1969. Neither is known for their quality journalism and high-brow opinions but they both remain lucrative parts of the Murdoch empire. Much to the disgust of the establishment, he also bought *The Times*. If he was to make his media concerns more

---
FOOD FOR THOUGHT

Problems begin when you don't clarify mutually agreed rewards and benefits for a project *before* it starts. When you have a project to complete, assign the right people to the team, ensure that everyone knows what is expected of them and how they will be measured against those expectations. Make everyone aware of the rewards and consequences of delivery and non-delivery and enforce those consistently. You don't need to be a bastard to succeed in business but you do need to be fair.

profitable and continue his quest for world domination, he needed to modernise the process and break the hold the unions had over newspaper production.

And that's exactly what he did. War broke out when he built a printing plant in Wapping, North London that did not require union labour. Despite picketing and increasingly violent industrial action, Murdoch quelled the disorder. He was shown through this action to be a decisive and ruthless leader, willing to do whatever it takes to get what he wants. His ambition was matched only by his debt. At one point in the early 1990s, he was $7 billion in the red, and counting, and it was only a last-minute deal at the start of 1991 that saved the business. His determination, ruthless pursuit of his goals and undeniable business acumen has made him one of the richest and most powerful men in the world.

He has his critics and certainly there are questions about how much Murdoch's own political views influence the quality and impartiality of information disseminating through his media network. Fox, his notoriously right-wing television network, was the subject of a controversial US documentary, *Outfoxed: Rupert Murdoch's War on Journalism*. But in terms of making his authority felt, enforcing his commands and quelling disorder, Rupert Murdoch has no contesters.

YOUR THOUGHTS

STUDY THE WELL-BEING
OF YOUR PEOPLE

Community partnerships, non-financial investments, and
profitable social responsibility can offer companies of all sizes
new ways to widen community relationships. All community
involvement is definitely good business.
- C WILLIAM VERITY JR, Industrialist

Just as no war can be won without the soldiers, no business can be successful without the people inside that business. It makes sense, therefore, to look after them and treat them well, yet those that do are the exception to the rule. Take Ben & Jerry's, for example. It was founded in 1978 by two ex-hippies after they'd taken a $5 correspondence course in ice-cream making! Although the business thrived, one of the ice cream duo – Ben Cohen – started to worry about being part of the business world. It was only when his friend suggested that they rewrite the rule book that he committed to what he still refers to as 'caring capitalism'.

In keeping with their hippy values, Cohen and fellow founder Jerry Greenfield wanted to create a socially responsible company that was built on mutual respect, not exploitation. And that's exactly what they've done.

They are famous for their treatment of staff and certainly don't overtax them. The 'Joy Gang', for example, is a group of employee volunteers

---

FOOD FOR THOUGHT

Is there any place for caring capitalism in your business? Encourage staff to suggest ways that your business could be more involved in the local community. The ideas can't involve just donating money but need to be innovative suggestions that involve the wider community and focus on how your business can assist others. Choose the best suggestion and implement it.

WORDS OF WISDOM

'Carefully study the well-being of your men, and do not overtax them. Concentrate your energy and hoard your strength', advises Sun Tzu. Keeping the troops well nourished and cared for, reserving their energy until needed and keeping them in good spirits is all part of a leader's role in securing victory.

whose task it is to 'keep work from becoming a grind'. With an annual budget of $20,000, the Joy Gang have introduced massage and pizza days, National Clash Dressing Day (where prizes are awarded for the worst dressed) and even a Barry Manilow Appreciation Day.

They have their critics, who think that their hippie values have simply been used to exploit a market, but the facts still speak for themselves. The Ben & Jerry's Foundation, founded in the mid-1980s to fund community projects, donated 7.5% of pre-tax profits to worthy causes (whereas the industry average is 1%). The not-for-profit initiative called '1% for Peace', aimed at redirecting 1% of the US defence budget to fund peace-promoting projects, has now evolved into a powerful body. Ben & Jerry's have done things differently and have proven that you can make money and be good corporate citizens at the same time. Listening to their staff, their customers (Cherry Garcia and Chunky Monkey were both flavours suggested by customers) and the community they operate in has meant that Ben & Jerry's are not only profitable but the people involved can sleep at night.

Despite Unilever's $326 million acquisition of Ben & Jerry's in 2000, the company has continued to exemplify the values of its founders and carefully study the well-being of not only their staff, but their customers and community too.

YOUR THOUGHTS

PUT YOUR BACK
AGAINST THE WALL

Those who want to succeed, will find a way;
those who don't, will find an excuse.
- LEO AQUILA, Activist

It is amazing what can be achieved when there is no escape. Whether born out of loyalty or desperation, employees gain focus and determination when business survival is at stake. *'Without waiting to be marshalled'*, they will give their last to the cause. *'If there is no place of refuge, they will stand firm.'*

Malden Mills is best known for two things: firstly, for inventing Polertec – a lightweight synthetic fleece made from recycled plastic bottles – and, secondly, for the response of owner and employees when Malden Mills burnt down in 1995.

Aaron Feuerstein had just returned home from a surprise seventieth birthday party when he heard about the fire. The only good news was that no one had died and the business was carrying $300 million in insurance. As some of the 2,400 employees gathered in a local gym to hear their fate, they were sure the factory would close – Feuerstein would take the money and retire. Instead he arrived, shook the snowflakes from his jacket, walked the length of the room and announced that not only would the factory be rebuilt in the same location, but also that all staff would continue to be paid while the

---

FOOD FOR THOUGHT

If you are facing a crisis, don't create options. Instead, gather your people together and put your cards on the table. Open the discussion up for feedback and suggestions on how best to tackle the problem. Look at the pros and cons of each and whittle your choices down. Make your final decision, and don't waver because it only serves to diminish confidence. Stand firm behind your choice and move forward.

> ### WORDS OF WISDOM
> Master Sun states, 'Throw your soldiers into positions whence there is no escape, and they will prefer death to flight. If they will face death, there is nothing they may not achieve. Officers and men alike will put forth their uttermost strength.' Close the exits and put your back against the wall.

construction took place. In addition, health benefits would continue and the staff would even receive their traditional Christmas bonus! The room erupted. There wasn't a dry eye in the house – including cynical news crews sent to cover the story.

Employees worked in round-the-clock salvage operations and Malden Mills was back to virtually full capacity within ninety days. Productivity and quality improved and the production of seconds dropped from 7% to 2%. Feuerstein became a national hero.

SRC, discussed in idea 20, also employed this philosophy. Facing bankruptcy, Jack Stack and twelve other managers bought the company from its owners, united the business and put their backs against the wall. They closed the exits and found reserves and passion that not only saved the business but also spawned a business philosophy – The Great Game of Business.

Sadly, Malden Mills didn't have such a happy ending. It never fully recovered but Feuerstein did the right thing and should be commended for it.

In the face of disaster, people will rally. But a word of caution: you only ever want that power on your side, never fighting against you. Sun Tzu says, 'When you surround an army, leave an outlet free. Do not press a desperate foe too hard.'

> ### YOUR THOUGHTS
>
>
>
>

ACKNOWLEDGE EMOTIONS

There can be no transforming of darkness into light,
and of apathy into movement, without emotion.
- CARL JUNG

For a long time, people were expected to come to work, leave their emotions at the door and do their job. The inescapable fact that they were human beings was steadfastly ignored. There was no room for outside life and certainly not messy personal problems and overt displays of emotion. Being a stoic workaholic was the only way to be and considered a prerequisite for promotion.

Today, that view is changing – even in the most unlikely places. Ford have never been held up as the model of employee liberation. The company's proud history was born instead out of industrialisation and automation. But even Ford are changing their ways. Nowadays, 360-degree employee performance reviews don't just include managers and colleagues, but family and friends too. Their evaluation is no longer restricted to their contribution to the business but their contribution to their family and local community. Ford's 'Total Leadership for the New Economy' is a direct response to the stress and overload associated with corporate life. They accept that people don't just live in a work vacuum but that they also have other responsibilities that need to be satisfied in order for them to be whole, happy and productive individuals.

FOOD FOR THOUGHT

Make it your task to find out more about your key people. You have to establish one piece of personal information about each member of your team that you did not read in their personal file. It might be the names of their kids, their favourite sports team or where they went on holiday; just find out something new. This will require talking to them as human beings.

WORDS OF WISDOM

Although he advocates the wise use of anger in battle, and how harnessing that emotion is necessary for success, Sun Tzu also states, *'On the day they are ordered out to battle, your soldiers may weep.'* This is his recognition of emotion as part of life and death – first human and then warriors.

A growing number of organisations are now convinced that if you can improve people's ability to understand and manage emotion, you will also improve performance, productivity, harmony in the workplace and customer communications – all factors that will immeasurably influence the bottom line!

Another unlikely candidate is American Express. More than two-thirds of Amex customers were declining to buy life insurance, even though their financial profiles suggested they needed it. After commissioning a work team to analyse the problem, the solution, while simple, took the financial giant into uncharted territory. The problem was emotional. Customers simply didn't want to talk about it and customer services staff were not equipped to handle such emotionally charged issues. The solution was to provide the sales team with focused training to increase their awareness of their own emotions. And the result apparently added tens of millions of dollars in revenues.

The interest in emotions in the workplace was greatly assisted by the work of Daniel Goleman. Publishing *Emotional Intelligence* in 1995, Goleman went on to write many more books on the subject. It was perhaps a case of right message, right time.

Business is a collection of people selling to a collection of people. People have emotions so treat them as such.

YOUR THOUGHTS

UNITE IN ADVERSITY

Never doubt that a small group of thoughtful, committed citizens
can change the world. Indeed, it is the only thing that ever has.
- MARGARET MEAD, Cultural Anthropologist

Master Sun points out that an army must learn to act as one streamlined unit, swift in response to danger from any angle. He emphasises this point by saying that if enemies can work together when in danger, surely one army should be able to work together. Yet, many a battle is lost because of lack of internal cooperation. In a business context, the message is equally relevant. Many businesses fold not because of external assault but through internal dispute and competing priorities.

A famous example of several rival businesses uniting in joint adversity to safeguard the future is the Swiss watch industry. United by one single priority – survival – it is an excellent demonstration of the power of cooperation between adversaries.

Think of Switzerland and it's not long before you think of clocks and watches. Yet, by the late 1970s, the prestigious industry was in big trouble. Cheap Asian competition had seen the Swiss slice of market share slip from 30% to just 9%. Swiss precision was always associated with the higher end of the market, yet that too was taking a battering because of fake imports.

FOOD FOR THOUGHT
Take a project that is currently stalled. Make a list of the people on the team and their responsibilities. If this is not clearly established, then this is the first point to tackle. If accountability is known and progress is still slow, individually discuss workload and commitment. It may be that team members are unsure where this project fits into existing priorities.

In a last ditch attempt to recover, leading Swiss manufacturers – who, until the crisis, had competed fiercely with each other in the same market – joined forces to form a consortium called ASUAG-SSIH. (Thankfully, this was later simplified with the help of businessman Nicolas Hayek to SMH.) They rightly felt it would be better to all go down fighting *together* than to die out individually with a whimper. The result was the Swatch.

Positioned as a disposable or replaceable fashion item, Swatch was the 'second watch' and was a direct assault on the cheaper end of the market. It was kept technically simple – this was not a timepiece that would be passed down through generations. There was a range of bright colours and ever-changing styles and designs. They were affordable and funky, and single-handedly put Swiss watch manufacturing back on top – the Swiss share increased to 50% of the worldwide market. Their continued innovation and design changes meant that Swatch watches even became collectors' items – so perhaps they will be passed down through generations after all.

None of this would have been possible had the entire industry not been in jeopardy. It is a striking example of what can be achieved between 'enemies' united by a common threat and a reminder of what therefore, should be possible between allies.

YOUR THOUGHTS

KEEP YOUR MOUTH SHUT

Loose lips sink ships.
- WWII SLOGAN

In business, too, it's considered advisable to play your cards close to your chest – as Gerald Ratner would no doubt attest. Ratner had joined the family business as a young man and became chief executive in 1984. He had taken the jewellery retailing business by storm and successfully built an impressive empire. The business grew under his stewardship and expanded from 130 stores and sales of £13 million to a public limited company with 2,500 stores, 25,000 employees and with sales of £1.2 billion.

It was no wonder, then, that he was invited to speak at the Institute of Directors. In 1991, in front of 6,000 business people – and, unfortunately for Ratner, several journalists – he delivered his now infamous speech. He joked, *'We also do cut-glass sherry decanters complete with six glasses on a silver-plated tray that your butler can serve you drinks on – all for £4.95. People say, "How can you sell this for such a low price?" I say, "because it's total crap."'*

FOOD FOR THOUGHT

Before you or anyone in your organisation gives a presentation about your business, especially to external suppliers, customers or the media, make sure it's vetted. Have a number of people read the presentation thoroughly to ensure that all the facts are correct and that nothing could be taken out of context or cause offence. The rule should be: 'If in doubt, take it out.' Getting a second opinion might ensure you don't make a costly mistake you live to regret.

The journalists present jumped on the story and within twenty-four hours, the business was in freefall. He wasn't drunk or nervous and had added the jokes in at the last minute – a decision that wiped an estimated £500 million off Ratner's share value. He was eventually forced out of the family business after a very difficult eighteen months.

Although his name is now synonymous with speaking out of turn, Gerald is by no means the only senior executive to 'do a Ratner'. Barclay's chief executive, Matt Barrett, suggested that astute consumers would do well to steer clear of his product. He admitted that he advised his four children not to 'pile up debts on their credit card'. Giving evidence to the Commons' Treasury Select Committee on credit cards, he said he did not use credit cards from Barclaycard because they were too expensive.

Or what about Topman brand chief, David Shepherd? He suggested his target market was, 'hooligans or whatever', whose purchase of a Topman suit would be, 'for his first interview or first court case'!

Even though it could certainly be argued that the statements were true, they were not sensible and, even if they were taken out of context, they serve as a reminder that good leaders stay quiet; they maintain a dignified silence and never mock their product or their customers, privately or publicly.

YOUR THOUGHTS

CHOOSE YOUR
ALLIANCES CAREFULLY

*Coalitions, though successful, have always found that
their triumph has been brief.*
- BENJAMIN DISRAELI

Whether it is the boardroom or a battlefield, alliances should be chosen carefully. In the late 1960s, the *News of the World* was owned by the Carr family. However, one of the Carrs wanted out and first replacement on the scene was Robert Maxwell. Ironically, considering the quality and reputation of their newspaper, this alliance was considered beneath them and Rupert Murdoch stepped up as their knight in shining armour.

Despite offering less than Maxwell, the deal was made – on the premise that the Carr family would remain involved, and Murdoch's promise not to seek outright control of the newspaper. Six months later, however, in a deceitful move that would have made Sun Tzu proud, Murdoch seized control. The Carr family had entered into an alliance without knowing Murdoch's true design – and obviously without getting that promise in writing!

IBM on the other hand used local guides very well when they wanted to move into the PC market. IBM, the most dominant computer firm

---

FOOD FOR THOUGHT

When negotiating with suppliers and forming alliances, be sure to specify everything that is crucial from your perspective. Problems occur because of what's not been specified rather than failure to comply with what has been. Don't take anything for granted and be sure to consider the worst-case scenario and make provisions to guard against it. Trusting people to keep their word is admirable but essentially foolish – especially if your alliance partner has read *The Art of War*.

on earth, was being shown up by new kids on the block – Apple. Frank Cary, IBM chairman at the time, ordered his people to produce an IBM-badged PC for August 1981. To do this, IBM would need to develop outside their core strength and, with time against them, IBM executives decided to hire in the expertise of some local guides – Intel and Microsoft.

Bill Gates *was* acquainted with IBM's design. IBM believed they were king of the hill and that Microsoft posed no threat – after all, what good was the Microsoft software without the IBM hardware? Bill Gates, though, recognised that the computer world was on the brink of a paradigm shift, a shift that would see software not hardware rule the roost. As a consequence, he was more than happy to form an alliance with IBM. He married his strategy with that of IBM and created a synergy that has made him the richest man in the world. IBM, on the other hand, did what many a business consultant would have advised them to do – focus on what they do best and outsource the rest. Ironically, it was Apple's refusal to make alliances and license their system that resulted in Microsoft's dominance.

Know what you want, be sure you know what your allies want and button that down in writing so there is no wriggle room on either side.

YOUR THOUGHTS

SILENCE IS NOT ALWAYS GOLDEN

Don't hide your strategy under a bushel.
Communicate it throughout your company. It's better
today to disclose too much than too little.
- JOEL E. ROSS, Business Author

In war, it's easy to see why this approach would be useful. And certainly, the philosophy has also been adapted well in business: it's known as the 'mushroom school of management' – keep them in the dark and feed them s*@t! Strangely, though, no single case study illustrates that this idea works in practice.

One company that seemed to take Sun Tzu's advice to heart is Exxon. On 24 March 1989, shortly after midnight, the oil tanker *Exxon Valdez* struck Bligh Reef in Prince William Sound, Alaska. There was 53,094,510 gallons of crude oil on board the *Valdez* and eleven million gallons gushed from her sides after the ship failed to return to shipping lanes after avoiding ice. At the moment of impact, Gregory Cousins, the ship's third mate, was at the helm. He was, however, not certified to pilot the tanker into those waters. There were accusations that the captain was drunk, although an Alaskan jury found him not guilty of that charge.

It was a disaster. Calm weather immediately after the spill could have greatly assisted immediate containment but the initial response didn't match the outlined measures in place to tackle such disasters.

FOOD FOR THOUGHT

Involve your people in both the good and the bad. If you don't tell them when there are problems, they will automatically assume the worst anyway and that is never constructive for the morale or performance of the business. So, share problems with your team. You never know, you might find a solution you'd never have thought of on your own.

> ─────────── WORDS OF WISDOM ───────────
> Master Sun suggests that you *'Confront your soldiers with the deed itself;*
> *never let them know your design. When the outlook is bright, bring it before*
> *their eyes; but tell them nothing when the situation is gloomy'*. So, when
> things are looking good, tell everyone – otherwise, keep quiet.

Deteriorating weather conditions made subsequent containment impossible. As for Exxon HQ, they didn't say a word: Exxon chairman, Lawrence Rawl didn't trust the media. When asked if he was going to be interviewed, he dismissed the question, saying he didn't have time for 'that kind of thing'.

Unfortunately for Rawl and the Alaskan environment, it was important enough to warrant the arrival of hoards of journalists who reported extensively not only on the devastation and lack of containment but also on the silence of the corporation responsible. It was only when President Bush declared the spill a 'major tragedy' that Exxon executives flew to Alaska to hold a press conference.

Spreading good news makes sense and certainly there is no need to shout about bad news but it's a little difficult to miss the equivalent of 125 Olympic-sized swimming pools of crude oil and a slick that stretched for 470 miles. It was hardly a secret.

Exxon did, of course, eventually come to the party but their silence cost them – and, more importantly, the fragile Alaskan environment – dearly. It took four years and $2.1 billion to clean up the mess.

Keeping quiet during challenging times may have worked for Master Sun in war but it's rarely positive in business.

> ─────────── YOUR THOUGHTS ───────────
>
>
>
>

WHEN THE ENEMY FALTERS
GO FOR THE JUGULAR

*I would rather be an opportunist and float than go to
the bottom with my principles around my neck.*
- STANLEY BALDWIN, Politician

Although Malden Mills, discussed in idea 42, was destroyed in one of the largest industrial fires in US history, it's a rare cause of business disaster. Certainly, arson is never mentioned in business schools. Hence, we should take Master Sun's advice in the wider context. He is reminding us that we need to be opportunists in business. Business can throw up some unlikely hurdles: sometimes, those hurdles are external, through changing legislation or shifting market conditions; sometimes, they may be the result of an accident or an internal error. Whatever the reason, you must realise that if you falter, your competition will step in. Conversely, if your competition falters, you must be on hand to capitalise on the error.

In 1985, the UK Central Public Health Laboratory made the connection between Farley's instant milk and salmonella. The company issued an immediate recall at a cost of £8 million but food scares relating to babies are hard to recover from. Farley's was put into liquidation and sold to Boots for £18 million.

FOOD FOR THOUGHT

If you don't already know, find out the sales split between old and new customers. Are new customers masking the loss of old ones? If so, you need to find out why the old are leaving: call ten former customers and ask them. Find out your areas of potential vulnerability and whether your system is failing either new or existing customers. If it is, fix it – before your enemies rush in.

WORDS OF WISDOM

Sun Tzu says, 'When fire breaks out inside the enemy's camp, respond at once with an attack from without'. Although he is not being metaphorical in this instance, he does earlier refer to the concept of capitalising on enemy errors: 'If the enemy leaves a door open, you must rush in.'

Boots tried to resurrect the brand but the health scare had effectively opened the door to Farley's competitors and two of their main rivals had rushed in. While Farley's was off the shelves, Cow & Gate and Wyeth both increased production to meet the gap left by their rival. By the time Farley's was ready to come back, their customers had gone elsewhere. Farley's was sold to Heinz for £94 million in 1994. Farley's Rusks, popular with generations of British kids, have even enjoyed a renaissance.

Paul Wieand had been the president of Independence Bancorp, a $2 billion bank outside Philadelphia, for four years and, at thirty-seven, was about to become one of the youngest big-company CEOs. He flew off to Paris with his wife to celebrate but while he was enjoying frogs legs and a nice drop of red, his competitor moved in for the kill. Although his rival had admitted defeat and congratulated Wieand before his departure, as Master Sun points out, 'peace proposals unaccompanied by a sworn covenant indicate a plot'. In Wieand's absence, his rival lobbied the board and got himself voted in as CEO. When he returned, Wieand was met with his own resignation letter and his high-flying corporate career was over. Thankfully, this jolt moved him on to a more rewarding path but it is a good reminder about the importance of closing all the doors behind you.

YOUR THOUGHTS

BEWARE THE EGO

Pride cometh before a fall.
- TRADITIONAL SAYING

In business, pride can often gather momentum and it's a short step between pride and arrogance. Any decisions that are influenced by anything other than solid business strategy and common sense are off to a bad start.

In idea 12, we looked at Dr An Wang. His bitter experience with IBM left him bruised – his pride mainly – and it profoundly affected his ongoing strategy, which was a significant factor in Wang's eventual demise.

Rubbermaid, the company briefly profiled in idea 25, was steered onto its iceberg because of a leader who was too arrogant and too proud to admit that what used to work wasn't working anymore. To be fair, CEO Wolfgang Schmitt inherited the business at a time when what worked did so – really, really well. Rubbermaid occupied a rarefied world of premium prices, ineffective competition and easy-going consumers. But when the business environment changed, their long-standing reputation for innovation was not enough. Bargain-price competition was gaining in quality and quickly replicating Rubbermaid's

---

FOOD FOR THOUGHT

The next time you make a decision and the people you tell look at you as though you've got two heads, consider your motivations for making that decision. Initial reactions of disbelief or confusion may indicate your choice needs review. If anger, pride, greed or boredom plays even the slightest role in your choice, step back and reassess the situation. Strive for an environment where your people are encouraged to share their ideas, thoughts and opinions. At least, that way you don't have to second guess everyone.

innovations. Despite being one of America's most admired companies, Schmitt's refusal to see the writing on the wall and company-wide arrogance meant that Rubbermaid was weakened to the point it was bought by a rival in 1998.

Schwinn Bicycle Company, another American icon, was brought to its knees by its own pride and arrogance in the face of a changing market. You know there might be bumps in the road ahead when the marketing executives declare, 'We don't have competition: we're Schwinn.'

And then there's Samsung, who were blindly led into the automotive industry by the absolute power of the group chairman, Kun-Hee Lee. It was a decision that many felt was based more on a personal interest and passion for cars than any sound business strategy. Not only was he chairman, he was also the largest shareholder in the company and as such always got what he wanted. It took three years of wrangling from the announcement until the first car rolled off the production line. Despite having no experience in automotive engineering, the cars were impressive. Rave reviews, however, made little impact on a slowing economy, overcapacity and a subsequent drop in demand. In early 1999, Samsung Motors went into receivership – largely put down to a billion-dollar whim!

Be it arrogance, pride or sheer bloody-mindedness, this type of decision making is short-sighted and foolish.

YOUR THOUGHTS

DO YOUR  DUE DILIGENCE

Knowledge is power.
- FRANCIS BACON

In business, knowledge is equally as important. Business success depends on myriad factors but, at the very least, an organisation must know its market, understand its customers, meet their needs and stay abreast of everything the competition is doing. Information is the foundation of sound decisions. If you don't have it, you're on a fast track to failure, as Australian insurance giant HIH found out.

On 15 March 2001, HIH went into liquidation in what represented one of Australia's biggest corporate collapses. As the liquidators tried to unravel the complexities of the business, their estimates of the loss rose sharply. By August of the same year, it was announced that HIH might be anything from between $3.6 billion to $5.3 billion in the red.

HIH did, by all accounts, make some major mistakes. An aggressive acquisition strategy in a crowded market didn't help. The most controversial of those acquisitions was FIA Insurance. In most situations like these, it is common practice to conduct thorough due diligence.

FOOD FOR THOUGHT

Review a current project in terms of what you genuinely know to be true. Seek to verify everything and eliminate assumptions from the data. Go over every piece of crucial information and challenge it with one question: 'What would happen to the company if these data were wrong?' If the answer is 'disaster', then you need to triple check its accuracy. If someone doesn't want to divulge information or verify authenticity, then be very suspicious.

This process basically ensures that what the company says about itself is true and accurate. However, in the case between Ray Williams' HIH and Rodney Adler's FIA, there was no due diligence conducted. Adler refused to allow it and instead HIH were forced to use publicly available information to assess the deal. Unfortunately, that public information did not disclose considerable under reserving of FIA's insurance business. HIH ended up paying $300 million for a business that was worth $100 million. Ray Williams had always been keen to acquire FIA and perhaps that desire clouded his judgement. It is certainly something we can be sure he reflected on while in prison for his part in the debacle. Following a Royal High Commission into the affair, several people were charged and sent to prison, including Rodney Adler.

It's difficult to imagine how the refusal to allow due diligence didn't set off alarm bells, and certainly HIH's demise was attributed to more than just the acquisition of FIA. But it is a reminder of the importance of gaining access to information and being able to verify its authenticity. Just as in war, business is a costly affair and Ray Williams' ignorance of his 'enemy's position' was indeed the 'height of inhumanity'. An estimated two million insurance policies were rendered worthless, having catastrophic repercussions on hundreds of thousands of innocent people – and it could have been avoided.

YOUR THOUGHTS

THE IMPORTANCE
OF FOREKNOWLEDGE

I skate to where the puck is going to be,
not where it is.
- WAYNE GRETZKY

As we have seen, accurate information is imperative for making good business decisions. Being able to view everything and everyone you come into contact with as a source of knowledge is a characteristic of a winning mindset. A brilliant modern-day example of achieving success way beyond the reach of ordinary men is Cheung Yan and her company Nine Dragons, China's largest maker of container cardboard.

After the company she worked with collapsed, she was faced with a choice of taking another salaried position or starting her own business. A seed of past experience fused with insights into the future and an empire was born. In her previous role, Yan had hit on the idea of trading waste paper after helping her mainland boss earn a tidy profit shipping paper from northern China to Guangdong. This piece of foreknowledge fused with her realisation that, as China's economy took off in the mid-1980s, demand for packaging for its growing exports would soar. Everything from DVD players to fridge freezers, outdoor furniture and hair dryers all had one thing in common – they all needed

---
FOOD FOR THOUGHT

Ask your managers to prepare half a SWOT document detailing what they consider to be the company's greatest opportunities and threats. To help envisage the potential challenges the business might face, have them imagine what the market you serve will be like in twenty years. Have them choose one opportunity and one threat and organise a brainstorm to discuss the results. Is anything actionable now?

a box to be packed in. Instead of jumping into the manufacturing frenzy, she was able instead to see a huge problem on the horizon and solve it ahead of time.

China had very limited timber resources of its own because most of the forests had been decimated to make way for a quarter of the world's population. The mills they did have used mostly straw pulp, which was environmentally devastating. China's problem was no paper. Across the other side of the world, the USA was creating vast quantities of paper waste. America's problem was too much paper. So Yan brought the two together and solved them both! She brought the unwanted paper from the US back to China, where it was recycled to begin its journey once again. This brilliantly simple solution has made Yan the richest self-made woman in the world.

By using her foreknowledge of trading paper, she was able to foresee a challenge that all China's manufacturers would encounter – affordable packaging. Not only does her wealth now eclipse the likes of J. K. Rowling and even Oprah Winfrey but she is employing thousands of people and doing something positive for the environment.

Great business leaders understand that information and ideas can come from anywhere. They see opportunities when others only see threats.

YOUR THOUGHTS

GATHER INFORMATION CAREFULLY

Integrity without knowledge is weak and useless,
and knowledge without integrity is dangerous and dreadful.
- SAMUEL JOHNSON

Gathering information about your competition is vital in determining the correct competitive strategy and staying ahead of the game. However, employing spies may work in war but perhaps McLaren and British Airways wouldn't recommend it in business.

In July 2007, McLaren escaped any immediate penalty after their chief designer was found in possession of a secret 780-page technical dossier of their arch rivals, Ferrari. Needless to say, Ferrari wasn't happy with the ruling. However, McLaren still faced a championship ban and were later clobbered with a massive fine. Ferrari would have been none-the-wiser had they not received a tip-off from the employee of a photocopy shop who had been asked to copy the document. How they knew what they were looking at is perhaps even more of a mystery!

Another business that got into deep trouble for the unethical collection of information is British Airways. When Richard Branson entered the skies in 1990 with Virgin Atlantic, he was British Airways' only UK competitor on long-haul routes. British Airways launched a secret war on Branson. Branson soon realised something was wrong and

---

FOOD FOR THOUGHT

One of the amazing things about the internet is that it offers anyone who is interested a global platform to broadcast their views. Make sure you routinely search newsgroups to find out when those views affect your company and when they affect your competition. Although it can never be taken as fact without verification, it does offer a unique insight into a world you may not be able to access any other way.

he became convinced there was a 'dirty tricks' campaign against him. Eventually, he was forced to go to court to prove it.

Evidence mounted against BA. Virgin, along with a few other small airlines, rented space from BA on their central reservation system, BABS. Unknown to Virgin, BA were gaining unauthorised access to Virgin flight details in an attempt to *manipulate the threads* and squeeze Virgin out. A secret unit called 'The Helpliners' was set up in Room 1278, a small windowless room inside Gatwick's north terminal. The information was fed into the 'Virgin Project' – the aim of which was to discredit Branson personally and do anything possible to win back customers. One of the tactics used was 'switch-selling'. BA staff would look at Virgin reservations and target upper-class passengers, either meeting them at their gate or calling beforehand and offering them incentives to move to British Airways.

In the end, justice was served and Virgin won the court case. BA was ordered to pay £610,000 to Virgin for libel; £500,000 to Branson personally. British Airways also paid the costs, which were reliably estimated at £4.5 million. And, most importantly for Branson, they were forced to apologise in open court.

Gathering information may well be the leader's *'most precious faculty'* but it must be carefully and ethically obtained.

YOUR THOUGHTS

CONCLUSION

*T*he *Art of War* has a reputation for advocating deception. It would certainly be easy to misinterpret it as providing permission for manipulation, an ancient thumbs-up for bad behaviour and proof that the end does always justify the means. Yet, that's not what is being said at all. The messages of duplicity are always tempered by an overriding caveat of *wisdom, sincerity, benevolence, courage* and *strictness*. Perhaps it's this apparent dichotomy that has fascinated so many for so long.

Sun Tzu talks frequently of the need to find balance between opposing forces. In doing so, he is recognising that a good leader may have to make hard decisions at times but that those decisions must come from a position of honour. There is no right answer, no magic bullet or sure-fire one-size-fits-all approach to success.

For every rule, there is always an exception. Nepotism didn't work for Dr An Wang when he put his son in charge. However, it did work for Mr Semler Snr when he passed his business to his son and stepped back: in his father's wake, Ricardo Semler has created an astonishing company that breaks just about every rule in the book. When Barnevik chose not to conduct due diligence in his cross-border merger with Brown Boveri, the merger moved ahead at breakneck speed and was hailed a triumph. Ray Williams of HIH did the same with FIA Insurance – a decision, among others, that landed him in prison.

There are no cast iron rules to business success but if you are able to understand what normally works and bring honesty, truth and integrity to your decision-making table, then you will be ahead of the game.

As a great leader, you must plan thoroughly, put your own house in order, find the right people and give them the resources and authority to execute their orders, choose a strategy and use cunning when necessary. You must learn to vary your tactics according to the situation. As Master Sun affirms so poetically, *'There are not more than five musical notes, yet the combination of these five give rise to more melodies than can ever be heard'*. You must gather momentum towards your goal and in times of negotiation, *'Begin by seizing something which your opponent holds dear, then he will be amenable to your will'*. But most of all, *'set up one standard of courage which all must reach'* and *'kick away the ladder behind'* you.

The Art of War is by all accounts a list of sentences and short paragraphs – ideas and experiences pulled together by Sun Tzu into thirteen areas of warfare. In the Giles translation, which is the predominant source in this book, there are 385 of those separate thoughts, although many are repeated.

Here, we've only focused on 52. In an effort to sooth your curiosity about the remaining 333, I'll finish the book by sharing a couple of my favourites.

'If forced to fight in a salt-marsh, you should have water and grass near you, and get your back to a clump of trees'. Or *'...country in which there are precipitous cliffs with torrents running between, deep natural hollows, confined places, tangled thickets, quagmires and crevasses, should be left with all possible speed and not approached.'*

As I could think of no meaningful parallel between business and salt marshes, I left that one out. And if you are a seasoned business person, you're probably more than familiar with confined places and tangled thickets of the 'rock and hard place' variety and, therefore, already know to leave them as quickly as possible!

REFERENCE MATERIAL

IDEA 1 - *The Art of War*, Sun Tzu. Translated from the Chinese by Lionel Giles, MA (1910), Chapter 1 – *Laying Plans* (5, 6).

IDEA 2 - *The Art of War*, Chapter 1 – *Laying Plans* (7, 8).
Brand Failures, Matt Haig, pp. 32, 139.

IDEA 3 - *The Art of War*, Chapter 1 – *Laying Plans* (9).
'Interview with Semco's business guru.' Reporter: Kerry O'Brien for *The 7.30 Report*, TV programme transcript.
'Maverick Leadership: A Radically Successful Approach to Management by O-mission.' Christine Miller interviews Ricardo Semler, *ReSource Magazine*, February 2007.
'Who's in charge here? No one', Simon Caulkin, *Observer*, 27 April 2003.
The Seven-Day Weekend, Ricardo Semler, pp. ix, 5

IDEA 4 - *The Art of War*, Chapter 1 – *Laying Plans* (10);
Chapter 4 – *Tactical Dispositions* (16).
Wikipedia on Jack Welch.
'"Create Candour in the Workplace," says Jack Welch', Lisa Vollmer, *Stanford Graduate School of Business Top Stories*, April 2005.

IDEA 5 - *The Art of War*, Chapter 1 – *Laying Plans* (16, 17).
Brand Failures, Matt Haig, p. 172.
The 75 Greatest Management Decisions ever made ...and some of the worst, Stuart Crainer, p. 182.
The Encyclopedia of Entrepreneurs, Anthony and Diane Hallett, p. 493.

IDEA 6 - *The Art of War*, Chapter 1 – *Laying Plans* (18, 19).
The 75 Greatest Management Decisions ever made, p. 147.

IDEA 7 - *The Art of War*, Chapter 1 – *Laying Plans* (20).
Brand Failures, Matt Haig, pp. 10–15.

IDEA 8 - *The Art of War*, Chapter 1 – *Laying Plans* (26).
Wikipedia, Hoover Free Flights Promotion.
'Hoovers Free Flights fiasco recalled', Angela Chan, BBC News 24, 13 May 2004.

IDEA 9 - *The Art of War*, Chapter 2 – *Waging War* (5, 19).
The 75 Greatest Management Decisions ever made, p. 101.
Brand Failures, Matt Haig, p. 119.
Brand Royalty, Matt Haig, p. 165.

IDEA 10 - *The Art of War*, Chapter 2 – *Waging War* (17).
Why Smart Executives Fail and what you can learn from their mistakes, Sydney Finkelstein, pp. 91, 100.

IDEA 11 - *The Art of War*, Chapter 3 – *Attack by Stratagem* (2),
Brand Failures, Matt Haig, pp. 105–110.

IDEA 12 - *The Art of War*, Chapter 3 – *Attack by Stratagem* (5).
'Cautionary tales of corporate confusion', Deborah Tarrant, *Australian Graduate School of Management Magazine*, 8 December 2005.
Why Smart Executives Fail, p. 110.
Gerry Harvey: Business Secrets of Harvey Norman's Retailing Mastermind, James Kirby, p. 69.

IDEA 13 - *The Art of War*, Chapter 3 – *Attack by Stratagem* (10).
Häagen-Dazs website
The 75 Greatest Management Decisions ever made, p. 24.

IDEA 14 - *The Art of War*, Chapter 3 – *Attack by Stratagem* (13).
Why Smart Executives Fail, pp. 79, 160.

IDEA 15 - *The Art of War*, Chapter 3 – *Attack by Stratagem* (15).
The 75 Greatest Management Decisions ever made, p. 56.
Brand Failures, Matt Haig, p. 213.
Why Smart Executives Fail, p. 249.

IDEA 16 - *The Art of War*, Chapter 4 – *Tactical Dispositions* (13, 14).
Why Smart Executives Fail, p. 196.
The 75 Greatest Management Decisions ever made, p. 20.
Brand Failures, Matt Haig, pp. 96, 84.

IDEA 17 - *The Art of War*, Chapter 5 – *Energy* (1).
The 75 Greatest Management Decisions ever made, pp. 104, 106.
'ABB: The Dancing Giant' by Kevin Barham and Claudia Heimer, review by Stuart Crainer, *Strategy & Business*, First quarter, 1999.

IDEA 18 - *The Art of War*, Chapter 5 – *Energy* (2).
CSR Performance Measures and the McDonald's System, 6 March 2007.

IDEA 19 - *The Art of War*, Chapter 5 – *Energy* (13, 15).

'Motorola: Can Chris Galvin save his family's legacy?' by Roger O. Crockett, *Business Week*, 16 July 2001.
Why CEOs Fail, David L. Dotlich and Peter C. Cairo, p. 49.
Why Smart Executives Fail, p. 64.

IDEA 20 - *The Art of War*, Chapter 5 – *Energy* (21).
The Great Game of Business website.
'Success Profiles – Creating Actionable Knowledge', website Springfield Remanufacturing Corporation.

IDEA 21 - *The Art of War*, Chapter 6 – *Weak Points and Strong* (1).
The 75 Greatest Management Decisions ever made, p. 190.
Brand Failures, Matt Haig, pp. 23, 24.

IDEA 22 - *The Art of War*, Chapter 6 – *Weak Points and Strong* (6, 7).
'The Story Behind the Sony Walkman' by Tom Hormby, *Orchard*, 15 September 2006.
'Sony history', Sony corporate website.
The Sydney Bridge Climb website.

IDEA 23 - *The Art of War*, Chapter 6 – *Weak Points and Strong* (25).
'A Better Way to Negotiate: Backwards' by James K. Sebenius, *Research & Ideas*, 26 July 2004: Harvard Business School Working Knowledge for Business Leaders website.
The 75 Greatest Management Decisions ever made, p. 106.

IDEA 24 - *The Art of War*, Chapter 6 – *Weak Points and Strong* (28).
Brand Failures, Matt Haig, p. 70.
'Blue food goes down the drain' by Parija Bhatnagar, CNN/*Money*, 20 June 2003.

IDEA 25 - *The Art of War*, Chapter 6 – *Weak Points and Strong* (31).
The 75 Greatest Management Decisions ever made, pp. 9, 49, 194.
Why Smart Executives Fail, p. 60.

IDEA 26 - *The Art of War*, Chapter 6 – *Weak Points and Strong* (33).
The 75 Greatest Management Decisions ever made, p. 99.
Brand Failures, Matt Haig, p. 15.

IDEA 27 - *The Art of War*, Chapter 7 – *Maneuvering* (20).
'Bonuses Aren't Just for the Bosses' by Rekha Balu, *Fast Company*, issue 41, November 2000.

IDEA 28 - *The Art of War*, Chapter 7 – *Maneuvering* (23).
Brand Failures, Matt Haig, p. 86.
Brand Royalty, Matt Haig, p. 16.
Why Smart Executives Fail, p. 196.

IDEA 29 - *The Art of War*, Chapter 7 – *Maneuvering* (25).
Why Smart Executives Fail, p. 68.
'Lead Softly, but Carry a Big Baton' by Jill Rosenfeld, *Fast Company*, issue 48, June 2001.
'Motorola: Can Chris Galvin save his family's legacy?' by Roger O. Crockett, *Business Week*, 16 July 2001.

IDEA 30 - *The Art of War*, Chapter 8 – *Variations in Tactics* (9);
Chapter 7 – *Maneuvering* (3).
Great Failures of the Extremely Successful, Steve Young, p. 2.
The 75 Greatest Management Decisions ever made, p. 132.

IDEA 31 - *The Art of War*, Chapter 8 – *Variations in Tactics* (12).
'The Top 25 Crimes of the Century: The Collapse of Barings Bank 1995' by Howard Chua-Eoan, *Time Magazine*.
Why Smart Executives Fail, p. 200.
Nick Leeson's official website

IDEA 32 - *The Art of War*, Chapter 9 – *The Army on the March* (24).
The 75 Greatest Management Decisions ever made, p. 97.
'Congressional Hearings, Enron Analysts: We Was Duped' by Dan Ackman, Forbes.com.
'The Enron Story That Waited To Be Told' by Howard Kurtz, staff writer, *Washington Post* website, 18 January 2002.
Why Smart Executives Fail, pp. 259, 268.

IDEA 33 - *The Art of War*, Chapter 9 – *The Army on the March* (35).
'Fiorina out, HP stock soars' by Paul R. La Monica, senior writer, CNNmoney.com, 10 February 2005.
'The Carly Chronicles: An Inside Look at Her Campaign to Reinvent HP' by George Anders, *Fast Company*, issue 67, January 2003.

IDEA 34 - *The Art of War*, Chapter 9 – *The Army on the March* (36).
'The Rise and Fall of Dennis Kozlowski' by Anthony Bianco, William Symonds and Nanette Byrnes, with David Polek in New York, cover story, *Business Week*, 23 December 2004.
Why Smart Executives Fail, pp. 209, 258.
'Profile: Jeffery Skilling', BBC *News*, 23 October 2006.
'Ebbers Agrees to Settle Shareholder Suit' by Carrie Johnson and Yuki Noguchi, 1 July 2005, washingtonpost.com.

IDEA 35 - *The Art of War*, Chapter 9 – *The Army on the March* (41).
'Schoolgirls' study nabs food giant' by David Eames, 24 March 2007, Nzherald.co.nz.

'Drugs giant faces court after girls' Ribena test' by Frank Thorne, *Scotsman*, 27 March 2007.

IDEA 36 - *The Art of War*, Chapter 9 – *The Army on the March* (43).
The 75 Greatest Management Decisions ever made, p. 139.

IDEA 37 - *The Art of War*, Chapter 9 – *The Army on the March* (45).
The Seven-Day weekend, Ricardo Semler, pp. 5, 32.

IDEA 38 - *The Art of War*, Chapter 10 – *Terrain* (18).
'Mint Condition', Anna Muoio, *Fast Company*, 30, November 1999.
The 75 Greatest Management Decisions ever made, p. 196.

IDEA 39 - *The Art of War*, Chapter 10 – *Terrain* (25).
'Gene Pool, Talent Pool: Hiring is all in the family' by Gina Imperto, *Fast Company*, issue 4, August 1996.
'Fun Fact Sheet' Southwest airlines website
'Using the Recession To Grow Your Company' by Renae Merle, staff reporter, *Wall Street Journal* online.

IDEA 40 - *The Art of War*, Chapter 10 – *Terrain* (26).
The 75 Greatest Management Decisions ever made, p. 154.
'Murdoch: Fox News does not favour Bush' by Claire Cozens and agencies, 26 October 2004, MediaGuardian.co.uk.

IDEA 41 - *The Art of War*, Chapter 11 – *The Nine Situations* (22).
Brand Royalty, Matt Haig, p. 167.

IDEA 42 - *The Art of War*, Chapter 11 – *The Nine Situations* (23, 24, 25); Chapter 7 – *Maneuvering* (36).
The 75 Greatest Management Decisions ever made, p. 86.
'The Mensch of Malden Mills', CNBNews.com, 6 July 2003.
'The Glow from a Fire' by Steve Wulf, *Time Magazine*, 8 January 1996.
The Great Game of Business website

IDEA 43 - *The Art of War*, Chapter 11 – *The Nine Situations* (28).
'Ford's Drive for Balance', Keith H. Hammonds, *Fast Company*, April 2001.
'How do You Feel?', Tony Schwartz, *Fast Company*, May 2000.

IDEA 44 - *The Art of War*, Chapter 11 – *The Nine Situations* (30).
The 75 Greatest Management Decisions ever made, p. 17.

IDEA 45 - *The Art of War*, Chapter 11 – *The Nine Situations* (35).
'Ratner prepares his return to the lions' den' by Bill Wilson, BBC business

reporter, BBC *News 24*, 29 March 2005.

'Barclays chief's gaffe recalls Ratner howler' by Bill Wilson, BBC business reporter, BBC *News 24*, 17 October 2003.

Wikipedia on 'Doing a Ratner'.

IDEA 46 - *The Art of War*, Chapter 11 – *The Nine Situations* (52).
The 75 Greatest Management Decisions ever made, p. 231.

IDEA 47 - *The Art of War*, Chapter 11 – *The Nine Situations* (57).
Brand Failure, Matt Haig, p. 103.
Exxon Valdez Oil Spill Trustee Council website
'Cautionary tales of corporate confusion' by Deborah Tarrant, *Australian Graduate School of Management Magazine*, 8 December 2005.

IDEA 48 - *The Art of War*, Chapter 12 – *The Attack By Fire* (6);
Chapter 11 – *The Nine Situations* (65).
Brand Failures, Matt Haig, p. 127.
'Farley's Rusks live on, say Heinz', BBC *News 24*, 4 June 2003.
'A Leader's Journey', Pamela Kruger, *Fast Company*, 25 May 1999.

IDEA 49 - *The Art of War*, Chapter 12 – *The Attack By Fire* (18).
Why Smart Executives Fail, pp. 31, 34, 43, 61, 63.

IDEA 50 - *The Art of War*, Chapter 13 – *The Use of Spies* (2).
'Case Study: HIH Insurance', Erisk.com.
'The demise of HIH: Corporate Governance Lessons' by Phillip Lipton, associate professor corporate law, *RMIT, Keeping Good Companies*, June 2003.

IDEA 51 - *The Art of War*, Chapter 13 – *The Use of Spies* (4).
'The cardboard queen who's bigger than Oprah' by Mary-Anne Toy, *Sydney Morning Herald*, 11 November 2006.
'Paper Queen', *The Economist*, 7 June 2007.

IDEA 52 - *The Art of War*, Chapter 13 – *The Use of Spies* (8).
'McLaren off hook in F1 spying row', BBC.co.uk, 26 July 2007.
Dirty Tricks: British Airways' secret war against Virgin Atlantic, Martyn Gregory pp. 78, 93, 250.

CONCLUSION - *The Art of War*, Chapter 1 (9), Chapter 5 (7), Chapter 11 (18, 32, 38), Chapter 9 (8, 15).

INDEX